INTERNATIONAL TRADE IN FILMS AND TELEVISION PROGRAMS

The American Enterprise Institute
Trade in Services Series

COMPETING IN A CHANGING WORLD ECONOMY PROJECT

Deregulation and Globalization: Liberalizing International Trade in Air Services — *Daniel M. Kasper*

Global Competition in Financial Services: Market Structure, Protection, and Trade Liberalization — *Ingo Walter*

International Trade in Business Services: Accounting, Advertising, Law, and Management Consulting — *Thierry J. Noyelle and Anna B. Dutka*

International Trade in Construction, Design, and Engineering Services — *James R. Lee and David Walters*

International Trade in Films and Television Programs — *Steven S. Wildman and Stephen E. Siwek*

International Trade in Ocean Shipping Services: The United States and the World — *Lawrence J. White*

When Countries Talk: International Trade in Telecommunications Services — *Jonathan David Aronson and Peter F. Cowhey*

International Trade in Services: An Overview and Blueprint for Negotiations — *Geza Feketekuty*

International Trade in Films and Television Programs

Steven S. Wildman

Stephen E. Siwek

An American Enterprise Institute/Ballinger Publication

Ballinger Publishing Company, Cambridge, Massachusetts
A Subsidiary of Harper & Row, Publishers, Inc.

International Standard Book Number: 0-88730-240-8

Library of Congress Catalog Card Number: 87-26913

Printed in the United States of America.

Library of Congress Cataloging-in-Publication Data

Wildman, Steven S.
  International trade in films and television programs.
  (American Enterprise Institute series on trade in services)
  Bibliography: p.
  Includes index.
  1. Motion-picture industry—United States.   2. Television industry—United States.
3. Motion-pictures, American—Marketing.   4. Television programs—United States—
Marketing.   5. Motion-picture industry—Finance.   6. Television programs, Foreign—
Finance.   7. Foreign trade and employment—United States.
I. Siwek, Stephen E.   II. Title.   III. Series.
PN1993.5.U6W494   1988
384'.83   87-26913
ISBN 0-88730-240-8

CONTENTS

List of Tables   ix

Editor's Foreword   xiii

Acknowledgments   xvii

Chapter 1   Introduction   1

Public Good Components of Films and Television
    Programs   2
Organization of the Monograph   7
Notes   11

Chapter 2   The World Film Trade and the U.S.
    Motion Picture Industry   13

World Trade Patterns   14
Foreign Films in the U.S. Market   22
Home Video Markets   26
The Importance of Foreign Markets to the U.S.
    Motion Picture Industry   26
Summary   33
Notes   35

**Chapter 3   International Trade in Television
Programs**   37

International Program Flows   37
Types of Programs Traded   46
The Role of Governments   49
Satellite Distribution of Television Programs 52
Cable Television   53
Notes   59

**Chapter 4   An Economic Model of Trade in Video
Products**   61

Previous Analyses of Trade in Video Products   62
The Model   67
Markets with Noncommercial Buyers   77
Notes   79

**Chapter 5   An Examination of Linguistic Markets:
Size and Potential**   83

The Potential of Linguistic Populations as Video
  Markets   84
Factors That Limit the Development of Video
  Markets   89
Notes   97

**Chapter 6   Barriers to Trade in Motion Pictures and
Television Programs**   99

Lack of Intellectual Property Protection   99
Quantitative Restrictions   105
Import Restrictions   106
Local Work Requirements   108
Discriminatory Taxes   108
Subsidies   109
Earnings Remittance Restrictions   110

Government Monopsony   111
Other Barriers   111
Observations   112
Notes   114

Chapter 7   The Political Economy of Nontariff
             Barriers to Trade in Video Products   117

Reasons for Barriers   117
Effects of Trade Barriers   119
The Relationship Between NTBs and Video Piracy   125
Notes   126

Chapter 8   Trade Agreements, Intellectual Property
             Agreements, and the Media Industries   129

GATT   129
OECD Codes   134
Film Industry Exceptions in GATT and OECD   136
European Economic Community   137
Other Models   141
The Berne and UCC Agreements on Intellectual
    Property   142
EEC Copyright Provisions   144
Other Copyright Agreements   145
Notes   147

Chapter 9   Conclusions and Recommendations   153

Matching Strategies to Barriers   153
The Most-Favored Nation Principle   156
Goods vs. Services   157
Market Access, Right of Establishment, and
    National Treatment   158
Other Concepts   161
Culture, Intellectual Property, and Trade Reform   163
Notes   164

Appendix A Film Import and Production Statistics for
            Ninety-Two Countries   169

Appendix B A Model of Trade in Films and
            Television Programs   177

Notes   183

Index   185

About the Authors   193

LIST OF TABLES

1–1	Global Prices for U.S. Television Films	5
2–1	Summary of Film Imports and Production for Sixty Countries	15
2–2	Distribution of Sales of Films by Nine Major Film-Exporting Nations	16
2–3	Attendance Shares of American Films in Eight European Markets	19
2–4	Attendance Share of U.S. Films in the Cinema Market of Four EEC Member States	19
2–5	*Variety* Estimates of Theatrical Box Office Revenues by Country of Origin in France	20
2–6	*Variety* Estimates of Market Share for the West German Film Market	20
2–7	*Variety* Estimates of Highest Grossing Film Releases in Italy	21
2–8	*Variety* Estimates of Film Rentals and Releases in Japan: Major Distributors	22
2–9	*Variety* Estimates of All-Time Highest Grossing Theatrical Releases in Spain	23
2–10	*Variety* Estimates of Highest Grossing Film Releases in Buenos Aires	24
2–11	*Variety* Estimates of U.S. Film Releases by Type of Release	25
2–12	Household Penetration of VCRs	27
2–13	World Video Cassette Recorder Population by Region	29

2–14	Video Cassette Distributor Market Shares, 1985	30
2–15	U.S. Motion Picture Industry Worldwide Theatrical Revenue Summary, 1984	31
2–16	Media Shares of U.S. Motion Picture Industry, 1984	31
2–17	Trends in Film Rental Revenues for U.S. Major Distributors Since 1963	32
2–18	U.S. Major Distributors' Film Revenue Rentals in 1975 and 1984	33
2–19	AFMA Member Companies' Theatrical Revenues from Foreign Markets	34
3–1	Estimated Television Receivers in Use	38
3–2	TV Overspill in Europe	39
3–3	Percentage of Imported Television Programs in 1973 and 1983	42
3–4	Growth in Foreign Television Program Syndication Revenues	45
3–5	Distribution of Programs by Region and Category	47
3–6	European Economic Community: Origin of Films Shown on Television in 1981	48
3–7	Ownership of Television Broadcasting Systems: Global Summary, 1983	49
3–8	Annual Radio and Television License Fees per Household in EEC Countries, 1983	51
3–9	European Households Wired to Cable Systems and Master Antennae, 1984	54
3–10	European Cable Television	56
5–1	A Comparison of Linguistic Populations	85
5–2	Production Costs of Feature Films	88
5–3	A Comparison of Television Advertising and Commercial Television Signals in the United States and Europe	92
6–1	Summary of Trade Barriers in Video Products	100

6–2	MPEAA Estimates of Market Shares Achieved by Pirated Videocassettes	103
6–3	MPEAA Estimates of Origin and Destination of Unauthorized Videocassettes	104
A–1	Film Production and Imports	170

EDITOR'S FOREWORD

The American Enterprise Institute's *Trade in Services Series* represents an important step toward creating the policy alternatives necessary to enhance the international competitiveness of American services.

The series is part of a larger, continuing AEI project, *Competing in a Changing World Economy*. Launched in 1983, this project has produced a wealth of publications, seminars, and conferences, analyzing the most significant policy challenges confronting U.S. policymakers in the areas of international trade and finance, science and technology policy, and human capital development.

Early in the project, we concluded that the United States would be successful in its drive to initiate a new round of trade negotiations with the other major trading nations, under the auspices of the General Agreement on Tariffs and Trade (GATT). We also chose to concentrate our resources on the new issues that would be placed on the table in that round: trade in services, intellectual property, and trade-related investment. In September 1986, at Punta del Este, Uruguay, the United States and the other members of GATT did indeed reach an agreement to launch a new multilateral round of trade negotiations, the Uruguay Round. Trade in services, along with intellectual property and investment issues, was included on the agenda. Hence, over the next several years negotiators in Geneva and top policy officials in all the major trading nations will face the formidable task of forging trading rules for these new issues.

In the area of services, a number of countries, including the United States, have produced individual, national studies of service trade liberalization. Yet government and private-sector officials agree that these studies are only a first step, and that substantial research remains to be done in key service sectors before major policy questions can be answered regarding a new service trade regime.

Designed to fill this policy gap, *Trade in Services* brings together eleven outstanding writers who have committed their expertise to analyzing the seven key service sector industries:

- Aviation—Daniel M. Kasper, Harbridge House

- Banking—Ingo Walter, Graduate School of Business Administration, New York University

- Construction—James R. Lee, American University, and David Walters, Staff Economist, Office of the U.S. Trade Representative

- Professional services—Thierry J. Noyelle and Anna B. Dutka, Conservation of Human Resources, Columbia University

- Shipping—Lawrence J. White, Member, Federal Home Loan Bank Board, on leave from the Graduate School of Business Administration, New York University

- Telecommunications: Information and Data Processing— Jonathan David Aronson, School of International Relations, University of Southern California, and Peter F. Cowhey, Department of Political Science, University of California at San Diego

- Telecommunications: Motion Pictures, Television, and Prerecorded Entertainment—Steven S. Wildman and Stephen E. Siwek, Economists Incorporated

In addition, Geza Feketekuty, of the Office of the U.S. Trade Representative, has written an overview volume for the series.

All of the books in the series embody two main goals: first, to analyze the dynamics of international competition for each of the seven industries, identifying existing and potential barriers to trade; and second, to formulate and assess policy approaches for opening service markets through an umbrella service agreement and subsequent individual sector agreements in GATT.

A related goal is to disseminate the results of our research through conferences and seminars, televised forums, and a variety of publication formats. We aim to make our findings known to government officials, trade experts, the business and financial communities, and concerned members of the public. To that end, during 1987 we convened major conferences in London, Geneva, and Washington, and in early 1988 the team of authors traveled to Tokyo and Singapore. Thus, as with all AEI projects, we have sought to ensure that the studies not only make a significant contribution to scholarship but also become an important factor in the decision making and negotiating processes.

In addition to the authors, who have produced outstanding books, we would like to thank John H. Jackson, Hessel E. Yntema Professor of Law at the University of Michigan, and Gardner Patterson, who for many years served in the GATT Secretariat. Both of these men provided invaluable help and guidance as advisers to the project.

—Claude E. Barfield
Coordinator
Competing in a Changing World Economy

ACKNOWLEDGMENTS

We would like to thank Claude Barfield of AEI for his support and continued dedication to this project. We would also like to thank William Nix, Norman Alterman, and Fritz Attaway of MPAA and Jonas Rosenfield of AFMA for their kind assistance in aiding our understanding of a complex and dynamic industry. Geza Feketekuty, Gardner Patterson, John Jackson, and the participants in the Trade-In Services Project made significant contributions to chapters 8 and 9. Among our many research assistants, we would especially like to thank Molly Minnear, Katherine Leupold, Kim Cronenwett, and Helen Reinecke. Meg Garretson, Monika TinWin, R. Townsend Davis, and Scott Shaw also provided valuable assistance. To Cindy Walton, Denise Andrews, and Ingrid Jones, we want to state our appreciation for countless hours of typing on the seemingly endless drafts of this manuscript. Finally, we are grateful to our wives, Susan and Marilyn, for their continuing support and encouragement.

INTERNATIONAL TRADE IN FILMS
AND TELEVISION PROGRAMS

1

INTRODUCTION

World markets for films and television programs have long been critically important to U.S. producers and distributors.[1] Over the last thirty years, foreign markets have generally accounted for about one-half of major U.S. producers' total sales in these industries. The success of American films and television productions in world markets is indicated both by industry trade balances and by comparisons with other film- and television-exporting nations. In 1985 the U.S. film industry had a positive trade balance of around $1 billion.[2] The United States has historically exported more than three times the total television programming exports of the next three leading exporting nations combined.[3] Despite this success, however, foreign earnings for the U.S. film and television industries are reduced substantially by a variety of barriers to trade in foreign markets.

Trade problems encountered in the media industries fall into two general classes: governmentally imposed, nontariff barriers (NTBs) and various forms of film and video piracy. These problems greatly reduce American industries' revenues in many markets. Nontariff barriers include various quantitative restrictions, limitations on the repatriation of earnings, and discriminatory taxes. Perhaps even more important in terms of its effect on export earnings is video piracy. Producers' and distributors' losses due to piracy have increased enormously as a result of the growth of new copying and distribution technologies that have given pirates a technological edge they did not have before. The Motion Picture Association of America (MPAA) estimates that the American film industry's annual losses due to piracy may be as high as $1 billion.[4] While piracy is seldom promoted actively

1

by foreign governments, there is no doubt that in some markets it is not discouraged and may even be tacitly approved.

Nontariff barriers to trade in films and television programs are part of a larger pattern of impediments to trade in services. Service providers in many industries encounter trade problems that cannot be addressed in a comprehensive multinational trade forum such as the General Agreement on Trade and Tariffs (GATT). GATT deals with trade and tariffs in goods rather than services. In recognition of the increasingly serious consequences of this omission, a consensus has emerged among U.S. policy-makers that trade in services should now be afforded the benefits of a comprehensive, multinational trade regime.

The development of a set of guiding principles to govern trade in services is an extremely difficult undertaking. The tasks of both researchers and trade negotiators are complicated by definitional and measurement problems, which are characteristics of trade in most services. In addition, it is not entirely clear that the analytical principles appropriate to trade in goods apply equally to trade in services. For this reason, the American Enterprise Institute for Public Policy Research (AEI) commissioned a series of industry-specific books that address the problems encountered in applying trade concepts to individual service industries. In this book, which constitutes one in the series, we provide a largely economic analysis of international trade in films and television programs and examine the effects of barriers to trade in these products. The next section of this chapter introduces the concept of a public good, which is critical to understanding media products in general and media trade in particular. In the final section of this chapter, we outline the organization of the remainder of the book.

PUBLIC GOOD COMPONENTS OF FILMS AND TELEVISION PROGRAMS

A public good is a product or service for which "consumption by any one economic agent does not reduce the amount available for others in the community."[5] National defense is probably the most commonly used example of a public good. If it is provided for one, it is necessarily provided for all the citizens of a country. Contrasted with the nonexclusive nature of public goods are private goods for which consumption is exclusive. A ham sandwich is a private good. If Tom eats it, Bill cannot.[6]

If only because knowledge—as a public good—is required to produce them, most products and services combine both public and private elements. Trade laws and most studies of international trade deal primarily with products in which the private element is predominant. Media products in general, and films and television programs in particular, are distinguished by the relative importance of their public good elements in both production and consumption.

For films and television programs, the value of the product to consumers is determined almost entirely by such public good elements as the appeal of the story portrayed, the quality of the writing and acting, the perspective of the director, and the competence of camera crews and other technical personnel. The value of these elements to one individual is not diminished by the probability that other people have already seen the film or program.

If a product is a private good, the fact that each unit of the product can be consumed only once means that production and transportation costs place fairly strict and narrow bounds on the range of prices that the product may be sold for in different countries. As a rule, products will not be sold at prices that do not cover at least the combined costs of production and transportation. In addition, profit-seeking entrepreneurs will ship products from areas where prices are low to regions where they are high. Barring trade restraints, international trade will tend to equalize prices across nations once allowances have been made for differences in transportation costs.

The tendency for trade to equalize prices across nations does not apply to products that are primarily public goods like films and television programs. The owner of a film or television program does not benefit by restricting availability of his product in Country A just because he can sell it at a higher price in Country B. The fact that a film or program is seen in Country A does not diminish its value to viewers in Country B. Therefore, the price at which the film or program is sold in one country bears no necessary relationship to the sales and earnings it will generate in another country.[7] Each additional country in which the film or program is sold represents a net addition to total profits, as long as distribution costs are covered.[8] The fact that products like films and television programs, which are primarily public goods, can sell at widely varying prices in different countries is clearly evident in the lists of prices paid for television programs and films sold for television featured in such trade publications as *Variety*[9] (see Table 1–1). The variability in the prices that audience members pay to view films in the theater is illustrated by the range of average prices for cinema admissions for various countries. In 1984 the average theater admission price in the United States was $3.34.[10] By contrast, the average admission price in the Philippines was $1.25; in Ecuador, it was $1.20.[11] The prices a film or program commands in different countries depend primarily on the values placed on it by viewers and broadcasters in those countries.

The prices paid for films and television programs are affected by a large number of factors that vary among countries. Besides government policies, which are discussed in Chapters 6 and 7, such demographic characteristics as population and per capita income and the structures of domestic theatrical exhibition and television industries are probably the most important determinants of prices. One would expect per capita income to affect film earnings since individuals will be willing to spend more for cinema entertainment when their disposable incomes are higher. Similarly, broadcasters will be willing to spend more on programming for the wealthier, and thus more valuable as potential customers to advertisers, audience members. Prices for television programming should also be higher in countries with large populations than in less-populated countries since the potential audience will increase with population. Of course, the degree to which potential evidence is translated into television viewership and cinema attendance depends on the number of broadcast stations and theaters, a factor that varies considerably among countries.

Table 1–1. Global Prices for U.S. Television Films.

	Half-Hour Episode	Feature Film
Canada		
CBC	$14,000– 20,000	up to $300,000
CBC (French Net)	6,000– 9,000	up to 100,000
CTV Network	15,000– 20,000	up to 300,000
Latin America and Caribbean		
Argentina	1,000– 1,500	3,000– 6,000
Bermuda	30– 45	90– 150
Brazil	4,000– 6,000	15,000– 30,000
Chile	220– 375	6,000– 10,000
Colombia	800– 1,500	2,000– 5,000
Costa Rica	180– 210	1,200– 1,750
Dominican Republic	100– 150	225– 300
Ecuador	200– 300	1,000– 6,000
El Salvador	75– 90	550– 625
Guatemala	100– 125	600– 1,200
Haiti	50– 75	100– 200
Honduras	85– 90	300– 400
Jamaica	80– 95	300– 400
Mexico	1,000– 2,000	10,000– 50,000
Netherlands Antilles	55– 85	150– 340
Nicaragua	75– 85	300– 500
Panama	200– 215	800– 3,000
Peru	250– 300	1,800– 2,000
Puerto Rico	1,100– 1,250	6,000– 20,100
Trinidad and Tobago	130– 140	500– 560
Uruguay	800– 1,000	2,500– 5,000
Venezuela	800– 1,000	2,500– 5,000
Western Europe		
Austria	900– 1,400	2,700– 5,000
Belgium	1,250– 1,750	5,000– 21,000
Denmark	700– 900	3,500– 4,000
Finland	900– 1,000	3,500– 4,000
France	8,500– 10,000	30,000– 40,000
West Germany	8,500– 18,000	50,000– 59,000
	(undubbed)	(dubbed)
Gilbralter	40– 94	125– 300
Greece	700– 750	3,000– 3,750
Ireland	300– 350	1,200– 1,400

5

Table 1–1 continued.

	Half-Hour Episode		Feature Film	
Italy	6,000–	48,000	20,000–	75,000
Luxembourg	1,200–	1,500	5,000–	6,000
Malta	45–	50	150–	250
Monaco	400–	450	1,200–	1,700
Netherlands	2,000–	2,250	7,500–	8,500
Norway	900–	1,000	3,500–	4,000
Portugal	215–	500	1,200–	2,000
Spain	1,500–	2,500	7,800–	18,000
Sweden	2,100–	2,500	10,000–	40,000
Switzerland	1,500–	2,000	4,000–	9,000
United Kingdom	12,000–	14,000	60,000–3,000,000	
Eastern Europe				
Bulgaria	200–	250	500–	1,000
Czechoslovakia	400–	600	2,000–	3,000
East Germany	750–	1,500	6,000–	10,000
Hungary	200–	300	1,300–	1,800
Poland	150–	375	1,000–	1,600
Rumania	200–	450	1,000–	1,800
USSR	120–	300	6,000–	8,000
Yugoslavia	175–	500	1,100–	2,000
Middle East and South Asia				
Cyprus	30–	75	100–	275
Egypt	400–	600	1,750–	2,500
India	500–	600	12,000–	20,000
Iran	500–	750	3,000–	4,000
Iraq	350–	500	1,200–	2,000
Israel	400–	500	1,200–	4,000
Kuwait	450–	500	1,750–	2,000
Lebanon	175–	200	800–	900
Saudi Arabia	650–	800	3,000–	3,200
Syria	70–	275	150–	1,250
Africa				
Algeria	90–	100	no sales	
Kenya	45–	60	110–	150
Nigeria	1,000–	1,500	5,000–	6,000
Zimbabwe	100–	125	250–	300
South Africa	1,250–	1,800	5,000–	7,500
Zambia	100–	115	350–	425

Table 1–1 continued.

	Half-Hour Episode		Feature Film
Far East			
Australia	NA	NA	75,000–500,000
Hong Kong	600–	850	6,500– 10,000
Japan	6,000–	7,000	60,000–200,000
South Korea	750–	1,000	up to 25,000
Singapore	300–	500	1,000– 1,700
Malaysia	400–	850	1,500– 3,400
New Zealand	625–	700	1,800– 3,000
Philippines	250–	600	3,000– 12,000
Taiwan	300–	400	4,000– 20,000
Thailand	500–	750	2,400– 3,000

Source: "Global Prices for TV Films," *Variety*, April 23, 1986, p. 58.

The importance of the public good components of films and television programs, combined with the development of new copying and distribution technologies, explains why piracy has become a critical barrier to trade in films. Videocassette recorders (VCRs) have made duplication of films and television programs easy and inexpensive, and satellite distribution and commercial cassettes have made them more accessible. Because the cost of duplication is low relative to the cost of producing the creative product, pirates can profit by selling illegal copies of films and television programs at prices that film and program producers and their authorized distributors would not find remunerative.

ORGANIZATION OF THE BOOK

The remainder of this book is organized as follows. Chapter 2 describes the basic patterns of world trade in motion pictures, documenting several important relationships. First, we establish that international trade in motion pictures is dominated by the productions of U.S. companies, followed distantly by films from other major industrialized democracies, and then by films from Hong Kong, India, and the Soviet Union. Films from the United States have historically accounted for very large shares of total film revenues in foreign theatrical markets, and sales in these markets are critical to the financial health of the U.S. film industry. Finally, foreign films, particularly foreign language films, achieve only limited success in the U.S. market. Similar relationships appear to characterize the rapidly emerging home video markets.

Chapter 3 provides an overview of trade in television programming. The close structural similarity of trade patterns in television programs to those in films is documented. Productions from the major industrialized democracies, especially the United States, dominate the trade in television material. The chapter also includes brief descriptions of institutions that have influenced the trend toward television program transmission by orbital satellites.

An economic model explaining the documented patterns of trade in films and television programs is presented in Chapter 4. The model predicts that films and programs produced in languages with large and wealthy native-speaking populations will have large budgets and greater inherent audience appeal than will films and programs produced in other languages. The audience appeal purchased through larger budgets is an advantage in international competition.

The strength of American films and television programs in world markets can therefore be explained by the fact that the English-speaking market for video products has much greater spending power than do markets comprised of other linguistic populations. Somewhat paradoxically, American media products would not be disproportionately represented in other countries were it not for the natural preferences of domestic audiences for films and programs in their native tongues. In competing for the large English-language audience, American firms produce motion pictures and television programs with an inherent audience appeal that is high enough to compensate for the handicap of having been filmed in a foreign tongue to viewers in most other countries. This is generally not the case for films and television programs produced in other languages. The size of the English-speaking market thus gives films and television programs produced in English an advantage in international competition (a "domestic opportunity advantage"). We explore the impact that this domestic opportunity advantage may have on film budgets and the number of filmmakers in different sized linguistic markets through examples.

In Chapter 5 we compare the various linguistic markets for video products. The English-language market is shown to be enormous in comparison to the others. Producers in English-speaking countries also benefit from having fewer governmental restrictions on the development of the commercial potential of domestic video industries, particularly television. Film and television producers in many non-English-speaking countries would benefit considerably if government restrictions on commercial television were relaxed. Larger budget, higher quality programs and films, which would be more competitive internationally and at home, would be produced if commercial restrictions were eased.

The trade barriers that are currently faced by the U.S. motion picture and television program industries are described in Chapter 6. We conclude that video piracy in its various forms is among the most widespread and serious of these problems. In addition, we list and describe in detail the more traditional non-tariff barriers, including screen and import quotas, restrictions on repatriation of film earnings, local work requirements, discriminatory taxes, and subsidized competition.

Political economy theories that explain the existence and form of trade barriers are reviewed in Chapter 7. In addition, trade barriers' potential effects on the industries that produce films and television programs are explored in some detail. The consequences of trade barriers for exporters of U.S. video products may be divided into two conceptually distinct effects. The direct effects of barriers are fairly obvious. A dubbing tax, for example, transfers money from the film's producer to the government imposing the tax, thereby reducing the producer's earnings. The indirect effects are less obvious. In the case of the dubbing tax, producers may respond to lowered potential earnings on films by producing fewer and less expensive films. Lower budget films attract smaller audiences, both in the domestic and foreign markets. Earnings from traded films and programs will therefore decline even further due to reduced quality and output. While the indirect effects of a single country's barriers are probably not large, the cumulation of the indirect effects of the barriers of many countries is potentially quite large. The direct and indirect effects of both NTBs and copyright enforcement problems are examined in some detail in the chapter. We argue that the problems of NTBs and piracy cannot be separated.

Chapter 8 provides an overview of the major trade agreements and intellectual property agreements that are relevant to future trade negotiations in media industries. These include GATT, various codes promulgated by the OECD, findings of the EEC, the Berne and Uniform Copyright Conventions, and specialized agreements such as the Geneva Phonogram Convention of 1972. Several of these agreements single out films and television for special treatment. Principles and concepts that are contained in existing multinational agreements and can be applied profitably in future negotiations on trade in services are identified and discussed.

We set out conclusions and recommendations for policy-makers concerned with trade in the film and video industries in Chapter 9. The chapter starts with an assessment of what can be achieved given the realities of the world trade in media products. We evaluate the prospects for making significant progress in liberalizing trade in films within the framework of such established institutions for trade negotiations as GATT. In addition, we review the menu of options currently available to U.S. producers and distributors who encounter difficulties in securing access to foreign markets.

Our first recommendation is that the scope of GATT be formally extended to provide a forum for negotiations regarding non-tariff barriers and intellectual property issues. In recognition of the importance of the domestic opportunity advantage of U.S. products, we recommend that, in exchange for a reduction in trade barriers, negotiators consider reductions in U.S. tariffs and barriers for industries in which other nations may have a comparative advantage. However, we also highlight the importance of foreign restrictions on media market size. We describe how changes in foreign regulatory policies for media industries may reduce the relative advantage of U.S. producers but still produce benefits for the video industries of both the host country and the United States.

NOTES

1. Jean Luc Renaud and Barry R. Litman, "Changing Dynamics of the Overseas Market Place for TV Programming," *Telecommunications Policy 9*, no. 3 (September 1985): 249.
2. U.S. Congress, Office of Technology Assessment, "Trade in Services: Exports and Foreign Revenues Special Report," OTA-1TE-316 (Washington D.C.: U.S. Government Printing Office, September 1986), p. 89.
3. Tapio Varis and Kaarle Nordenstreng, *Television Traffic: A One-Way Street?* (Paris: Boudin/UNESCO, 1974), p. 30.
4. Tom Bierbaum, "Piracy War: Slow-Win Situation: Newer Technologies Offset MPAA Gains," *Variety*, November 13, 1985, p. 1.
5. Jack Hirshleifer, *Price Theory and Applications*, 2d ed., (Engelwood Cliffs, N.J.: Prentice-Hall, 1980), p. 539.
6. For a more extensive discussion of the importance of the distinction between public and private goods to understanding the economics of media industries, see Bruce M. Owen, Jack H. Beebe, and Willard G. Manning Jr., *Television Economics* (Lexington, Mass.: Lexington Books, 1974,), pp. 15–16.
7. There is the possibility that a high price for a movie or television program in one country may make piracy of the film or program more likely. If pirate versions of the film or program showed up in another country, its value in legitimate commercial channels in the second country would be reduced. We deal with the implications of piracy in some detail later in this book.
8. This contrasts with a private good for which at least marginal costs of production would have to be covered.
9. International television prices are no longer an annual feature in *Variety*. In a personal communication to the authors, Sid Silverman, editor and publisher of *Variety*, pointed out that the prices published by *Variety* were not precise and were subject to some debate. We cite the *Variety* data to illustrate the range of country-to-country variation in prices; for this purpose it is more than adequate.

10. Richard Gertner, ed., *1986 International Motion Picture Almanac*, 57th ed. (New York: Quigley Publishing Company, 1986), p. 35A.
11. Ibid., pp. 694, 700.

2

THE WORLD FILM TRADE
AND THE U.S. MOTION
PICTURE INDUSTRY

S tudies of industries and trade must begin with factual descriptions of industry structures and patterns of trade. In this chapter we describe important relationships that characterize international trade in films and examine the U.S. motion picture industry as a player in the world film market.

We look at three aspects of the world film trade: numbers of films crossing national boundaries, impacts of imported films on domestic film markets and audiences, and financial flows associated with the trade in films. In turn, we examine three different types of data that correspond to these three aspects of trade: data based on counts of films produced and imported on a country-by-country basis, data on the audiences and box office revenues generated by foreign and domestic films for a variety of countries, and data on financial payments.

The fact that three different types of data must be used to describe the film trade and its consequences is largely due to the public good characteristics of films described in Chapter 1. If films were standard commodities like steel or oil, one could expect a close relationship between numbers of films imported, domestic consumption (audiences), and financial payments. The importance of the public good component in films attenuates considerably the linkage between these aspects of trade. Admission prices and cinema audiences vary dramatically from market to market, and a film that is wildly successful in one country may bomb in another. For these reasons we need to use the different types of data listed above to describe adequately the dimensions and implications of the world trade in films.

WORLD TRADE PATTERNS

Numbers of Films Produced and Traded

The annual tallies of production and import statistics that are compiled by UNESCO are by far the most comprehensive source of data on the numbers of films produced and traded worldwide. These statistics cover a majority of the countries that are members of the United Nations. The figures reported in Tables 2–1 and 2–2 are based on UNESCO statistics for ninety-two nations and territories. The data set underlying these tables is worth examining for its own sake and is presented in Appendix A.

The UNESCO data clearly show that most countries produce relatively few films and import most of the films viewed by their citizens. A few countries produce large numbers of films. Not surprisingly, domestically produced films generally account for a larger proportion of the films shown in the major film-producing nations. Table 2–1 summarizes the gross import and production statistics for sixty countries for which both production and import figures are available.[1] (The United States is not represented in this table. While U.S. filmmakers consistently produce more than 300 films annually, there are no statistics on numbers of films imported into the United States.)

The negative relationship between domestic film production and domestically produced films as a fraction of total films is quite obvious in Table 2–1. Most of the observations fall on or near a diagonal that connects the upper left corner with the lower right corner of the table. Half of the countries represented in Table 2–1 produced 20 or fewer films annually; about two-thirds produced 40 or fewer. Forty-five countries, 75 percent of the sample, had an annual production of 60 films or fewer. Only one of these countries had domestic productions accounting for more than 30 percent of films shown there. Just four countries produced more than 150 films. Domestic productions accounted for over 30 percent of total films shown in all four countries and for more than 60 percent of the total in three of them. Table 2–1

14

Table 2-1. Summary of Film Imports and Production for Sixty Countries.

Production as Percentage of Total Films	Annual Number of Domestic Productions										Percentage of Sample Countries
	0–20	21–40	41–60	61–80	81–100	101–150	151–200	201–300	301+	Total	
0–5	22	0	0	0	0	0	0	0	0	22	37
6–10	6	2	0	0	0	0	0	0	0	8	13
11–20	1	7	2	0	2	1	0	0	0	13	22
21–30	0	3	1	2	1	2	0	0	0	9	15
31–40	0	0	0	0	0	1	1	0	0	2	3
41–50	0	0	0	0	0	0	0	0	0	0	0
51–60	0	0	0	0	1	0	1	0	0	2	3
61–70	1	0	0	0	0	0	0	0	1	2	3
71–80	0	0	0	0	0	0	0	0	1	1	2
81–100	0	0	0	0	0	0	0	0	1	1	2
Total	30	12	3	2	4	4	2	0	3	60	100
Percentage of sample countries	50	20	5	3	7	7	3	0	3	100	

Source: UNESCO, Statistical Yearbook, Paris: UNESCO, 1984, Table 8.2, and Statistical Yearbook, 1985, Tables 9.1 and 9.2. The film import and production statistics underlying this table are from the late 1970s and early 1980s. See Appendix A for a discussion of the data set underlying this table.

Table 2–2. Distribution of Sales of Films by Nine Major Film-Exporting Nations.

	Number of Countries Distributed in	Number of Countries in which Sales are Number 1 Source[a]	Number of Countries in which Sales are 1 of Top 3 Sources[a]	Number of Countries in which Sales Account for at Least 5% of Imported Films
United States	79	56	77	79
France	68	5	36	40
Italy	71	2	39	52
India	42	6	23	23
USSR	55	10	17	28
United Kingdom	69	1	19	33
West Germany	56	0	8	15
Japan	46	0	5	7
Hong Kong	53	4	19	28

Source: UNESCO, *Statistical Yearbook*, 1984 (Paris: UNESCO, 1984), Table 8.2, and *Statistical Yearbook*, 1985, Tables 9.1 and 9.2. The film import and production statistics underlying this table are from the late 1970s and early 1980s. See Appendix A for a discussion of the data set underlying this table.

a. For cases in which two countries tied for the position of top source of imported films, both were assigned the rank of number two. Similarly, if two or more countries tied for the third position, none were counted among the top three sources of imported films. For this reason the total for the "Number 1 Source" column is less than the number of countries in the sample.

almost certainly under-represents the proportion of all the countries that belong in the upper left cell—those whose domestic productions account for less than 5 percent of all films released within their borders annually. Twenty-seven countries provided import statistics but no production statistics. Countries providing only import statistics are almost all either very small countries (or protectorates) or poorer Third World nations; they are usually both. Film production could very easily have been zero, and was almost certainly very low, for these countries. (Australia is the only obvious exception to this generalization.)

From the figures presented in Table 2–1, it would be reasonable to surmise that the few countries producing films in large numbers would be the major suppliers of films to the majority of countries that import most of their films. This is, in fact, the case. For the late 1970s and early 1980s data from which Tables 2–1 and 2–2 were constructed, UNESCO identifies the nine countries listed in Table 2–2 as major film-exporting nations. (Hong Kong is a British Crown colony, but we will refer to it as one of the major film-exporting countries for expositional convenience.) Percentages of total imports accounted for by films from these countries are given for eighty-seven of the ninety-two countries in the UNESCO data set. From these import percentages, four indices, or measures, of the relative importance of the major film-exporting nations were constructed. For each of the major exporting countries we calculated: the number of countries in which its films were distributed; the number of countries in which it was the number one source of imported films; the number of countries in which it was one of the top three sources of imported films; and the number of countries in which it accounted for at least 5 percent of imported films. The United States ranks a clear number one on all four measures. The second and third indices are probably the best indicators of the importance of the United States as a supplier of films relative to the other major film-exporting countries. The United States is the largest supplier of imported films in fifty-six of the eighty-seven countries (64 percent) in the sample. The Soviet Union, as principle supplier for nine countries (10 percent), and France, as the most important supplier for seven countries (8 percent), are a distant second and third. The United States is one of the three most important suppliers of imported films in seventy-seven countries—twice as many as either Italy or France, which are second and third by this measure. The UNESCO statistics clearly show the United States to be by far the world's most important supplier of films for international trade.

Regional trading relationships and linguistic and political ties are not reflected in Tables 2–1 and 2–2 but are evident in the underlying data and are even more obvious in older, more detailed UNESCO statistical reports on films.[2] Mexico is an important source of imported films in Latin America. While French films are imported by countries throughout the world, they are particularly popular in Haiti and former French colonies inNorthern Africa. Films from Hong Kong are imported in all regions of the world, but they generally make up larger shares of imports in Southeast Asian countries than elsewhere. Importation of Indian films is concentrated in Africa, Southeast Asia, and the Arabic countries of the Middle East. Egypt is a predominant supplier of films to countries in northern Africa, the Middle East, and the Soviet Union.

Table 2–2 shows that films produced in the larger European countries are exported throughout the world. However, films from these countries make up a significantly larger share of all the films within Western Europe. The primary importers of films from the Soviet Union are other Eastern bloc countries and countries with Communist or Marxist governments elsewhere in the world.

Attendance and Revenue Figures

With the exceptions of Western Europe and Japan, data on audiences and revenues generated by imported films are spotty at best. What data are available, however, strongly reinforce the previously established picture of the United States as the dominant global supplier of imported films.

The shares of attendance figures for eight European countries reported in Table 2–3 demonstrate the importance of U.S. films to European cinema audiences. Cinema attendance for U.S. films ranges from 30 percent for Italy to 80 and 92 percent for the Netherlands and the United Kingdom respectively. The comparative importance of films from European nations and other countries is indicated by the attendance share reported in Table 2–4. Films produced by U.S. companies accounted for 47 percent of the combined cinema audience in France, Italy, the United Kingdom, and West Germany. A distant second and third were Italy, with 24 percent, and France, with 17 percent. Film rental data, while less complete, tell the same story and can be seen from the *Variety* statistics for France, West Germany, and Italy (reported in Tables 2–5, 2–6, and 2–7).

Table 2–3. Attendance Shares of American Films in Eight European Markets.

Country	Percent
United Kingdom	92
Netherlands	80
Greece	70
Denmark	60
West Germany	50
Belgium	45
France	45
Italy	30

Source: European Parliament Working Document 1-504/83, PE 76.975/Final July 15,

Table 2–4. Attendance Share of U.S. Films in the Cinema Market of Four EEC Member States.[a]

Country	Number	Percent
U.S. films	334 million	47
Italian films	169 million	24
French films	118 million	17
British films	58 million	8
German films	24 million	3
Rest of world[b]	—	1
Total attendance of four markets	704 million	100

Source: European Parliament Working Document 1-504/83, PE 76.975/Final July 15, 1983, p. 23.

a. France, Italy, United Kingdom, and West Germany.

b. Films from other EEC countries are included in the "Rest of world" figures.

The degree of commercial success currently realized by American films in Europe is not a recent phenomenon. European nations were imposing restrictions on U.S. distributors as early as the 1920s. American films have probably enjoyed popular acceptance at or near present levels at least as far back as the mid 1950s.[3]

Table 2–8 provides estimates of film revenues and number of releases in Japan by major distributors during the years 1983

Table 2–5. *Variety* **Estimates of Theatrical Box Office Revenues by Country of Origin in France (first quarter 1985).**

Country	Dollar Amount of Receipts	Percentage of Total
France	47,786,000	49
United States	35,525,000	37
United Kingdom	7,442,000	8
All Others	6,247,000	6
Total	97,000,000	100

Source: Ted Clark, "French B.O. Took 1st-Qtr. Dive; Gallic Pics Suffered the Most," *Variety*, June 12, 1985, p. 35.

Table 2–6. *Variety* **Estimates of Market Share for the West German Film Market.**

Country	1979	1980	1981	1982	1983
West Germany	16.8%	9.3%	18.7%	11.7%	13.0%
United States	39.5	54.9	52.9	49.0	52.0
France	12.3	6.4	6.7	14.7	NA
Italy	11.4	13.8	8.4	13.8	NA
United Kingdom	13.0	6.9	6.6	5.1	NA
All Others	7.8	8.7	6.7	6.5	NA
Total	100.0%	100.0%	100.0%	100.0%	NA

Source: "German-Speaking Market at a Glance," *Variety*, March 7, 1984, p. 336.

and 1984. As the table indicates, CIC earned $47.1 million in film rentals during 1984, or approximately 18 percent of the total dollars earned in Japan that year. Combining CIC's 1984 revenue with the $15.4 million achieved by Columbia, the $13.6 million realized by Warner, and the $2.7 million earned by Twentieth Century Fox brings the total revenues for U.S. distributors in Japan to $78.8 million, or 30 percent of the total Japanese rentals, for 1984. (The comparable total for 1983 was 30.2 percent.)

The sparse data from smaller film markets also suggest dominance by U.S. releases. Table 2–9 lists the all-time highest grossing theatrical releases in Spain. No Spanish titles appear until the rank of nineteen, with *Los Santos Inocentes* achieving

Table 2–7. *Variety* **Estimates of Highest Grossing Film Releases in Italy (1984 through April 14, 1985).**[a]

Film	Origin	Distributor	Dollars
Nothing Left to Do but Cry	Italy	COL	2,890,000
Ghostbusters	United States	COL	2,725,000
Indiana Jones	United States	UIP	2,210,000
The Two Carabinieri	Italy	COL	2,106,000
The Neverending Story	West Germany	Medusa	2,030,000
Police Academy	United States	WB	1,820,000
He's Worse Than Me	Italy	CDE	1,645,000
Woman in Red	United States	CDE	1,560,000
Phenomena	Italy	Titanus	1,350,000
Thus Spoke Bellavista	Italy	UIP	1,266,000
Total			19,602,000
U.S. share ($)			8,315,000
U.S. share (%)			42.4%

Source: "Top 10 Italian Grossers," *Variety*, May 1, 1985, p. 301.

a. Based on first-run release in twelve key cities.

$2,681,000 in box office revenues. The first fifteen, and sixteen of the top eighteen, films originated in the United States. (*Clockwork Orange* is a British film and *Gandhi* is a British-Indian-American production.) *E.T.*, the highest grossing film, generated $9,546,000 in box office revenues. Finally, the fifteen all-time highest grossing films released in Buenos Aires are listed in Table 2–10. American films, with attendance of 2,346,518, accounted for 55.1 percent of the total.

Of course, films from almost every country will generate much larger shares of their own domestic box offices than they achieve on a worldwide basis. The United States is no exception in this regard; this means that comparisons of data from national markets will understate the relative importance of the United States in the global film trade. Unfortunately, very little data on national film exports are available on a regular basis from countries other than the United States. However, a comparison

Table 2–8. *Variety* **Estimates of Film Rentals and Releases in Japan: Major Distributors.**

Company	1983 ($ millions)	1984 ($ millions)	Number of Films Released in 1984
Toei	55.4	55.9	24
CIC	60.3	47.1	46
Toho	33.4	32.4	19
Toho-Towa	36.6	29.9	17
Shochiku	24.8	24.0	15
Columbia	13.7	15.4	12
Warner	5.3	13.6	15
Nippon Herald	34.4	13.2	23
Shochiku Fuji	14.2	12.8	13
Nikkatsu	13.5	12.3	65
Joy Pack Film	3.7	3.1	2
Fox	14.2	2.7	8
Total	309.5	262.4	259

Source: "Japan Film Distribution," *Variety*, May 1, 1985, p. 395.

of 1983 U.S. film export earnings of over $1.5 billion[4] with export figures of $35 million and $30 million for France and Italy, respectively, for the same year[5] provides perspective on the relative importance of films from the United States in world trade. France and Italy were probably the second- and third-largest film exporters in 1983.

FOREIGN FILMS IN THE U.S. MARKET

The dramatic success achieved by U.S. films in overseas markets contrasts sharply with the performance of foreign-made and foreign-language films in the United States. Although a large number of foreign films are released in the U.S. market, they tend, on average, to achieve limited box office success. Table 2–11 lists the numbers of foreign films released in the United States during the last few years. About 20 percent of film releases are subtitled imports; between 4 and 7 percent are English-dubbed movies.

Table 2–9. *Variety* **Estimates of All-Time Highest Grossing Theatrical Releases in Spain.**

Rank	Film	Box Office Revenue
1	E.T.	$9,546,000
2	Raiders of the Lost Ark	4,649,000
3	Superman	4,137,000
4	Gremlins	4,053,000
5	Star Wars	3,760,000
6	Tootsie	3,645,000
7	Indiana Jones	3,540,000
8	Police Academy	3,500,000
9	Return of the Jedi	3,269,000
10	Gone with the Wind	3,256,000
11	Superman, Part 3	3,182,000
12	Officer and a Gentleman	3,046,000
13	Superman, Part 2	2,924,000
14	Midnight Express	2,860,000
15	Grease	2,842,000
16	Clockwork Orange	2,787,000
17	Kramer vs. Kramer	2,759,000
18	Gandhi	2,692,000
19	Los Santos Inocentes	2,681,000
20	El Crimen Je Luenca	2,634,000
21	Jaws	2,632,000
22	Airplane	2,628,000

Source: "Alltime B.O. Champs in Spain," *Variety*, May 1, 1985, p. 410.

With the exception of films produced in English, few if any of these foreign films attain major box office prominence. For example, the *1985 International Television Almanac* lists forty-four foreign films released in the United States by independent distributors during the period September 1983–August 1984,[6] twenty-five of which were either dubbed or subtitled in English. Nevertheless, of these twenty-five films, only two, *Les Comperes*, a French film subtitled in English, and *El Norte*, a Spanish-language film with English subtitles, generated U.S. rentals in excess of $1 million in 1984. According to *Variety*, these films produced 1984 rentals of $1 million and $2 million,

Table 2–10. *Variety* **Estimates of Highest Grossing Film Releases in Buenos Aires.**

Rank	Film	Origin	Attendance
1	Porky's	United States	630,858
2	Camila	Argentina	504,711
3	Terms of Endearment	United States	335,058
4	Police Academy	United States	303,633
5	La Cage aux Folles	France	286,402
6	La Traviata	Italy	276,998
7	Le Marginal	France	241,877
8	Last Tango in Paris	United States	234,705
9	Jaws 3	United States	216,175
10	Breakdance	United States	214,239
11	Last American Virgin	United States	208,945
12	Darse Cuenta	Argentina	208,257
13	Indiana Jones	United States	202,905
14	Bingo Bongo	Italy	201,733
15	Fanny & Alexander	Sweden	190,089
Total			4,256,585
U.S. share			2,346,518
U.S. share (%)			55.1%

Source: "Top Grossers in Buenos Aires," *Variety*, March 27, 1985 p. 7.

respectively.[7] By way of comparison, the film *E.T.* generated domestic revenues of $187.8 million in 1982.

Distribution by a major U.S. studio does not appear to increase the box office appeal of foreign-language films in any appreciable way. In the period September 1983–August 1984, the U.S. majors distributors' "classics" divisions released twenty-eight films, twelve of which were dubbed or subtitled in English. Of these twelve, again only two films, *Carmen*, a Spanish release, and *Entre Nous*, a subtitled French film, achieved rentals above $1 million.[8]

Data from the 1970s tell a similar story. The Commission of the European Communities studied the European film industry and reported that "in the first fifty [films] of the five 'Variety' lists of Box Office Winners for 1975–1979 (that is, 250 films in

Table 2–11. *Variety* **Estimates of U.S. Film Releases by Type of Release.**[a]

Film Source	1970	1982	1983	1984	1985
Major distributors					
U.S.-made releases	109	105	111	103	90
British Commonwealth imports	21	8	10	11	11
Subtitled imports	17	14	16	13	7
English-dubbed imports	8	0	1	0	0
U.S. focus/specialized	7	8	4	1	2
Total Majors	162	135	142	128	110
Mini-Major distributors					
U.S.-made releases	35	22	18	44	55
British Commonwealth imports	6	3	2	4	2
Subtitled imports	7	0	3	4	7
English-dubbed imports	3	0	2	1	1
U.S. focus/specialized	0	0	1	1	0
Total Mini–Majors	51	25	26	54	65
Independent distributors					
U.S.-made releases	89	70	78	79	118
British Commonwealth imports	22	24	27	29	32
Subtitled imports	98	44	48	68	80
English-dubbed imports	23	14	11	26	15
U.S. focus/specialized	64	18	31	28	33
Total Independents	296	170	195	230	278
Grand Total	509	330	363	412	453
Percent share of subtitled imports	24	18	18	21	21
Percent share of dubbed imports	7	4	4	7	4

Source: Lawrence Cohn, "Indie Pics Pace 1st-Quarter Releases," *Variety*, April 2, 1986, p. 38.

a. Excludes reissues, hardcore pornography, untranslated ethnic-circuit imports, and martial arts imports.

all), twenty-six were national films of foreign countries. Twenty-four of these were British, all of which were distributed in the United States by American companies."[9]

Not surprisingly, English-language films originating outside the United States do much better than foreign language imports in American theaters. However, even imported English-language films account for only a small fraction of box office revenues in the United States.

HOME VIDEO MARKETS

Home video's growth from insignificance to a major entertainment industry is undoubtedly the biggest story of the 1980s in video entertainment. Unlike cable television, which has experienced slow growth in most countries outside North America, the explosion in VCR ownership has been worldwide (see Tables 2–12 and 2–13). While a variety of forms of programming are distributed via videocassettes, motion pictures account for a majority of cassette rentals and sales. Not surprisingly, the major motion picture distributors have also become involved in the distribution of videocassettes.

Data on shares of revenues from videocassettes for films by country of origin are not available. However, data on the shares of leading firms in cassette distribution in five European countries (Table 2–14) show that the major U.S. film distributors, or the cassette distribution organizations in which they participate, are also important distributors of cassettes. The combined shares of U.S. cassette distributors account for between 40 and 60 percent of cassette rentals and sales in each of these five countries.

THE IMPORTANCE OF FOREIGN MARKETS TO THE U.S. MOTION PICTURE INDUSTRY

In 1984 the U.S. motion picture industry achieved worldwide theatrical sales of more than $5.3 billion. While the majority of these revenues was generated by theatrical rentals, $1.2 billion came from videocassette sales, $600 million from pay television, and over $500 million from U.S. network, syndication, and foreign television rentals (see Table 2–15). The relative impor-

Table 2–12.   Household Penetration of VCRs (percent).

Country	1983	1984	1985	Projected 1986
Argentina	NA	1.4	2.3	3.7
Australia	NA	33.0	45.0	50.0
Austria	3.5	8.5	10.5	12.0
Bahrain	NA	60.0	53.1	58.0
Belgium	4.0	9.7	14.9	18.7
Brazil	NA	NA	3.5	5.0
Canada	4.5	15.0	26.0	31.0
Chile	NA	2.5	2.8	3.3
China	NA	NA	1.1	1.9
Colombia	NA	NA	22.0	27.7
Cyprus	NA	NA	15.6	18.9
Denmark	8.0	17.0	23.0	28.5
Ecuador	NA	10.0	10.6	12.8
Egypt	NA	NA	6.6	8.8
Finland	3.0	13.0	20.2	24.0
France	4.7	10.0	14.0	17.0
Germany	10.0	21.0	22.0	26.0
Greece	0.6	4.0	6.9	8.3
Hong Kong	NA	30.0	40.0	57.0
Iceland	NA	NA	52.7	62.5
India	NA	11.3	31.8	43.3
Indonesia	NA	19.3	15.0	16.4
Iran	NA	13.4	17.7	20.9
Iraq	NA	16.5	23.3	27.0
Ireland	5.0	19.0	22.0	27.0
Israel	NA	NA	51.2	60.4
Italy	0.8	2.5	3.0	5.0
Japan	13.4	40.0	35.0	43.0
Jordan	NA	21.0	15.2	15.9
Kenya	NA	NA	11.0	16.0
Kuwait	NA	NA	71.0	73.5
Lebanon	NA	NA	57.0	62.3
Luxembourg	NA	NA	26.4	34.0
Malaysia	NA	NA	40.3	50.8
Mexico	NA	2.3	7.1	11.3
Netherlands	9.7	NA	29.0	35.0
New Zealand	NA	8.8	20.0	28.0
Nigeria	NA	NA	26.3	38.1
Norway	11.0	15.0	25.0	33.0

Table 2–12   continued.

Country	1983	1984	1985	Projected 1986
Oman	NA	NA	81.0	89.0
Panama	NA	NA	36.0	46.6
Peru	NA	17.5	22.5	27.9
Philippines	NA	30.4	40.0	42.5
Poland	NA	NA	4.6	5.7
Portugal	0.5	NA	10.0	15.0
Qatar	NA	NA	59.2	62.6
Saudi Arabia	NA	23.8	37.7	44.1
Singapore	NA	43.0	60.0	65.0
South Africa	NA	11.1	16.3	20.3
Spain	2.6	9.5	13.8	18.4
Sweden	14.0	20.0	23.6	27.9
Switzerland	NA	15.0	20.9	25.0
Taiwan	NA	25.0	13.2	14.7
Thailand	NA	NA	9.1	10.6
Turkey	NA	NA	22.8	29.7
Uruguay	NA	NA	1.0	2.0
United Arab Emirates	NA	43.0	79.8	83.9
United Kingdom	15.0	36.0	40.0	46.0
United States	6.3	14.0	31.0	43.0
USSR	NA	NA	0.1	0.1
Venezuela	NA	NA	28.9	32.9
Zimbabwe	NA	NA	8.9	13.2

Source: Data for this table are from publications of the International Federation of Phonogram and Videogram Producers (IFPI), London. 1983 and 1984 statistics come from two IFPI annual review issues: Paul Mungo, ed., *IFPI 1983* (London: IFPI, 1983), p. 79 and David Laing, ed., *IFPI 1984* (London: IFPI, 1984), p. 56. 1985 and 1986 statistics are from IFPI, *Video Statistics 1985–1986* (London, IFPI, 1986), Table 2.

tance of foreign markets to U.S. film producers and distributors is illustrated in Table 2–16. As the table indicates, foreign revenues from all sources were $1.7 billion, almost 32 percent of the industry total. However, the relative importance of sales in the U.S. and foreign markets varies among media. For example, in 1984 film sales to foreign television broadcasters were only $135 million, just 8 percent of total foreign sales. By contrast, industry sales of more than $1 billion to U.S. television outlets comprised almost 28 percent of total U.S. revenue.

Table 2–13. World Video Cassette Recorder Population by Region (thousands installed at year end).

Region	1979	1980	1981	1982	1983	1984	1985	1986
EEC	704	1,748	4,020	8,463	12,936	17,205	21,977	30,249
Scandinavia	82	170	416	692	945	1,250	1,574	1,922
Rest of Western Europe	55	143	295	600	990	2,508	3,633	2,216
Western Europe	841	2,061	4,731	9,755	14,871	20,963	27,184	34,387
Eastern Europe	—	—	—	—	—	560	955	1,495
North America	1,155	2,050	3,510	5,755	10,300	18,708	31,783	45,579
Central America	30	50	85	135	295	673	1,255	1,988
South America	57	262	515	853	1,295	1,209	1,749	2,451
Africa	20	50	110	220	600	1,130	2,224	3,545
Middle East	137	412	721	1,153	1,630	2,195	2,680	3,148
Asia	84	141	316	545	1,150	1,145	1,890	2,865
Far East	1,295	2,235	4,055	7,140	11,565	16,655	22,560	28,435
Australia	45	102	265	635	1,245	2,010	2,715	3,335
World Total	3,664	7,363	14,308	26,191	42,951	65,248	94,995	127,228

Source: International Federation of Phonogram and Videogram Producers (IFPI). *Video Statistics 1985–1986* (London: IFPI, 1986), Table 1. Reprinted by permission.

Table 2–14. Video Cassette Distributor Market Shares, 1985 (percent).

Company	Belgium	Germany	Netherlands[a]	Spain	United Kingdom
CBS/Fox 5.0	—	8.0	10.0	8.2	
CIC Video	15.0	9.8	19.0	2.0	1.1
Cinema	11.0	—	—	—	—
Dubois HVP	10.0	—	—	—	—
Guild	—	—	—	—	3.3
MGM/UA	—	)	—	—	—
Disney	—	9.0	—	3.0	2.6
Vestron	—	)	—	—	1.2
Orion[b]	—	—	—	5.0	4.8
Polygram	—	—	—	2.0	2.7
RCA/Columbia	9.0	9.0	18.0	17.0	11.0
Thorn EMI	12.0	—	14.0	6.0	14.8
VMP	—	10.0	—	—	13.2
Warner Home Video	12.0	11.0	18.0	11.0	18.3
Others	26.0	51.2[c]	23.0	41.0	18.8

Source: International Federation of Phonogram and Videogram Producers (IFPI), *Video Statistics 1985–1986* (London: IFPI, 1986), Table 21.

a. 1st quarter 1985.

b. In Spain Orion is called Video 1000; in the United Kingdom it is called Rank (Orion/ABC/Touchstone).

c. German companies.

The current importance of foreign markets to U.S. filmmakers is not an aberration (illustrated in Table 2–17). The foreign component of U.S. majors' film rentals has ranged from over 50 percent in the early 1960s to approximately one-third in 1984.[10] The 1984 figure is significantly below the recent historical norm. It must be recognized, however, that much of the apparent decline in the importance of foreign sales reflects the strength of the U.S. dollar in 1984 versus the currencies in which most foreign box office revenues are denominated. From 1967 to 1984, for example, the dollar rose 127 percent against the British pound and 91 percent against the French franc. The dollar has fallen against most major currencies since 1984, and this should translate into a higher revenue share from foreign markets. In

Table 2–15.   U.S. Motion Picture Industry Worldwide Theatrical Revenue Summary, 1984 ($ millions).

Source	Estimated Revenue
Theatrical/Rentals	
Domestic	1,800
Foreign	1,100
Pay television	600
Videocassettes	
Domestic	750
Foreign	450
Network and syndication	410
Foreign television	135
Disc and other	75
Total	5,320

Source: Goldman Sachs Research, *The Movie Industry, The Big Picture: 1985*, March 11, 1985, Table 1.

Table 2–16.   Media Shares of U.S. Motion Picture Industry, 1984.

	Domestic Market		Foreign Markets	
	$ Millions	Percent	$ Millions	Percent
Theatrical rentals	1,800	49.5	1,100	65.3
Television[a]	1,010	27.8	135	8.0
Videocassettes	750	20.6	450	26.7
Disc and other	75	2.1	0	0
Total	3,635	100.0	1,685	100.0

Source: Goldman Sachs Research, *The Movie Industry, The Big Picture: 1985*, March 11, 1985, Table 1.

a. Includes network and syndication rentals as well as pay television transactions.

addition, film piracy, which has been assisted by recent technological developments such as the VCR and increased satellite transmission of television programming, has also taken a toll.

The identities of countries that are important purchasers of U.S. films change very little over time. Table 2–18 lists U.S.

Table 2–17.   Trends in Film Rental Revenues for U.S. Major Distributors Since 1963.

Year	U.S. Rental Revenue ($ millions)	Export Rental Revenue ($ millions)	Total Rental Revenue ($ millions)	Export Rental Share (percent)
1963	239	293	532	55.1
1968	372	339	711	47.7
1973	390	415	806	51.5
1974	546	495	1,041	47.6
1975	628	592	1,220	48.5
1983	1,300	838[a]	2,138	39.2
1984	1,310	654	1,964	33.3

Source: 1963–75 data from C.H. Sterling and T.R. Haight, *The Mass Media: Aspen Institute Guide to Communication Industry Trends* (New York: Aspen Institute and Praeger Publishers, Inc., 1977), Table 740-C; 1983 and 1984 data from A.D. Murphy, "Global Pic Rentals Tumbled 8% in '84: E.T. and Dollar Partly to Blame," *Variety*, June 12, 1985, p. 3.

a. Reflects results of Universal Pictures' 1982 release of *E.T.*, which entered foreign markets in 1983.

majors' rental revenues from the fifteen largest foreign markets for 1984. Also shown are the revenues for countries that were among the top fifteen markets in 1975. The stability of sales to foreign markets is quite apparent; with two minor exceptions, the same countries constituted the top fifteen markets in both years. The ranking among markets also changed very little over the nine-year period. This stability may be of considerable importance in reaching agreements to liberalize trade in services for the film industry since necessary assumptions about probable trade flows can be made on the basis of a reasonably reliable and consistent historical record.[11]

The activities of U.S. independent filmmakers are not documented as extensively as the majors'. However, a recent survey conducted on behalf of the American Film Marketing Association (AFMA) indicates the success achieved by U.S. independents in foreign markets. The results of this survey are summarized in Table 2–19, which disaggregates revenues from licensing for theatrical release by U.S. independent filmmakers

Table 2–18.   U.S. Major Distributors' Film Revenue Rentals in 1975 and 1984.

	1975 ($ millions)	1984 ($ millions)	Simple Percentage Change
Canada	63.2	111.0	75.6
Japan	56.6	77.0	36.0
France	52.1	69.5	33.4
West Germany	40.2	48.0	19.4
Italy	56.1	40.0	−28.7
United Kingdom	37.2	35.0	−5.9
Spain	32.5	33.1	1.8
Australia	37.0	33.0	−10.8
Mexico	17.0	17.6	3.5
Brazil	21.7	11.4	−47.5
South Africa	19.6	11.2	−42.9
Sweden	13.2	10.5	−20.5
Switzerland	8.0	10.2	27.5
Belgium	a	8.2	—
Taiwan	a	8.0	—
All Others	137.6	130.3	−.3
Total	592.0	654.0	10.5

Sources: A.D. Murphy, "U.S. Film B.O. at New Global Peak: Business Soars to $1.2 Bil, Up 17% Since '74," Variety, September 1, 1976, p. 1; "Top Markets for U.S. Pics, 1984," Variety, June 12, 1985, p. 3.

a. These countries were not among the major distributors' top fifteen markets in 1975.

in major markets around the world. The table shows a pattern of geographic distribution that, for the most part, parallels that of the major studios.[12]

SUMMARY

While there are considerable gaps in the data reviewed in this chapter, the important patterns that characterize international flows of films are quite clear. The most prominent structural feature of the international film trade is the dominant position of films from the United States. The largest Western European

Table 2–19. AFMA Member Companies' Theatrical Revenues from Foreign Markets ($ millions, 1984).

Europe	
United Kingdom	23.9
France	18.7
Germany/Austria	14.9
Italy	14.8
Spain	11.4
Other	27.8
Total	111.5
Latin America	
Mexico	4.5
Brazil	0.7
Venezuela	2.9
Other	11.9
Total	20.0
Far East	
Japan	18.4
Other	15.8
Total	34.2
Other	
Australia/New Zealand	20.9
South Africa	6.2
All Other	2.8
Total	29.9
Grand Total	195.6

Source: American Film Marketing Association (AFMA) poll byPannell, Kerr, Foster reported in Hy Hollinger, "Indie Foreign Sales Billion $ Business: Survey Sez AFM Top Marketplace," *Variety*, October 9, 1985, p. 40.

countries, India, Hong Kong, the Soviet Union, and Japan also merit recognition as significant international suppliers of films.

Regional trading relationships and political ties are reflected in the flows of traded films. While U.S. films are an important component of film imports almost everywhere, film exports from the other major exporting nations tend to exhibit more regional concentration. As a global film exporter, there is no close second to the United States.

Foreign sales are critical to the health of the U.S. film industry. In some years revenues from foreign sales and rentals account for as much as one-half of the industry's total. Regulations and events that affect the trade in films between the United States and other nations are therefore of vital interest to the success of the American motion picture industry.

NOTES

1. The UNESCO tables used as data sources underlying Table 2–1 do not always report both production and import statistics for the same year. For countries where production and import numbers from the same year were not available, the two closest years among the most recent seven or eight for which both an import and an export figure were available were employed. For this reason, and because not all countries reported import and production numbers for every year, no single year can be ascribed to the figures in the table.
2. UNESCO, *Statistics on Film and Cinema 1955–1977*, Statistical Reports and Studies No. 25, (Paris: UNESCO, 1981) lists Spain, Sweden, Egypt, and Mexico, as well as the countries listed in Table 2–2, as major suppliers of imported films. In addition, the data for these earlier years includes percentages of films supplied by lesser film-exporting countries. Percentages of films imported are provided only for the nine largest supplier countries in the UNESCO survey reports that are the basis of the first two tables of this chapter.
3. For a review of the history of American film exports to Europe, see T.R. Guback, *The International Film Industry: Western Europe and America Since 1945* (Bloomington: Indiana University Press, 1969); and T.R. Guback, "Hollywood's International Market," in *The American Film Industry*, ed. Tino Balio (Madison: University of Wisconsin Press, 1976), pp. 387–409.
4. Goldman Sachs Research, *The Movie Industry, The Big Picture: 1985*, March 11, 1985, Table 1.
5. Commission of the European Communities, *Promotion and Development of a European Programme Industry: Study of an*

Aid Scheme for Cinema and Television Co. Productions, Commission Working Paper, SEC (84) 1798, Final, November 16, 1984, p. 10.

6. Richard Gertner, ed., *1985 International Television Almanac*, 30th ed. (New York: Quigley Publishing Company, 1985), p. 313.

7. "Big Rental Films of 1984," *Variety*, January 16, 1985, p. 78.

8. *Entre Nous* produced $1.9 million in rentals while *Carmen* produced $1.4 million in the same year.

9. Andrew Filson, *The Distribution of Films Produced in the Countries of the Community* (Commission of the European Communities, 1980), p. 79.

10. The majors, that is, the largest U.S. film distributors, generally are members of the Motion Picture Association of America (MPAA) and the Motion Picture Export Association of America (MPEAA). In 1984 these companies were Columbia Pictures, Walt Disney/Buena Vista, Embassy Communications, MGM/UA, Orion, Paramount, Twentieth Century Fox, Universal, and Warner Brothers.

11. However, the emergence of videocassette piracy and its impact on foreign markets may well inject considerable volatility into the historically stable patterns of trade among U.S. filmmakers and foreign exhibitors.

12. The American Film Marketing Association (AFMA) survey also covers television and home video sales by the independents in foreign markets. The $196 million in theatrical sales, which is broken down by region in Table 2–19, was 52 percent of $375 million total theatrical sales by independents. Foreign television sales accounted for 16 percent of the total, and home video sales provided the remaining 32 percent.

3

INTERNATIONAL TRADE IN TELEVISION PROGRAMS

World trade in television programming is a large and growing component of total trade in media products. Given the dramatic growth in the worldwide television audience, this is not surprising (see Table 3–1). Increases in audiences and television rights payments for the Olympic Games dramatically illustrate the trend. In 1968 the worldwide audience for the Olympic Games in Mexico was estimated at 600 million.[1] Viewership for the 1984 Los Angeles games was 2.5 billion. Payments for television rights to the 1984 Olympics in Los Angeles totaled $287 million, nearly three times the $101 million paid for the 1980 games.[2]

In addition to the dramatic increase in the global television audience, growth in the world trade in television programming has been fueled by increasing use of new transmission and distribution technologies and by changes in official policies governing television in countries that are major television markets. Our objectives in this chapter are to provide as accurate a description of international programming flows as available data permit, to give some background on the role of governments in determining programming flows, and to examine the trade implications of the new technologies that have become an unstoppable force for change in the television industry.

INTERNATIONAL PROGRAM FLOWS

A number of factors complicate the task of identifying and describing patterns of trade in television programming; paucity

Table 3–1. Estimated Television Receivers in Use (thousands).

Region	1960	1965	1970	1975	1980	1983
Africa	122.4	562.2	1,205.9	2,473.5	6,052.2	9,825.7
Asia	7,064.0	19,330.4	27,427.5	37,723.3	60,572.1	71,278.0
Europe	20,973.0	74,352.2	125,254.8	169,081.0	245,251.0	261,744.0
North America	60,781.6	77,821.8	96,540.9	141,000.0	178,171.7	210,419.3
South America	2,110.5	5,510.8	12,570.9	18,909.6	27,456.0	30,898.0
Oceania	1,125.5	2,395.4	3,479.6	5,481.0	6,593.5	7,572.5
World total	92,177.5	179,972.8	266,479.6	374,668.4	524,096.5	591,737.5

Sources: 1960–75 data from UNESCO Division of Statistics on Culture and Communication, Office of Statistics, *Statistics on Radio and Television 1960–1976*, no. 23 (Paris: UNESCO, 1978), Table X; 1980–83 data from UNESCO, *Statistical Yearbook*, 1985 (Paris: UNESCO, 1985), Table 10.

of data is the most serious of these. Despite the growing importance and visibility of traded programming, data on programming flows are surprisingly incomplete—even less complete than those for films. This is partly because the trade in programming is still considerably smaller than the trade in films. Therefore, the financial incentives to collect data are not as strong. Also, it is probably significant that broadcasting is not a commercial enterprise in many countries.

Of course, the problems, discussed in Chapter 2, arising from the public good characteristics of the product make the interpretation of various measures of trade in television programming difficult; this is also the case for films. Program audiences and program prices calculated on a per-audience-member basis vary widely from country to country and from program to program. Therefore measures of import consumption (audiences), hours of imported programs, and financial payments for imported programming may not be closely correlated.

Cross-border broadcasting, or signal overspill, also complicates the task of correctly identifying importing and exporting countries (see Table 3–2). For example, if Luxembourg television purchases "Dallas" from its U.S. producers, and French and Belgian viewers watch the program on Luxembourg television, has "Dallas" been imported from the United States into Luxem-

Table 3–2. TV Overspill in Europe.

Country	Type of Overspill
Austria	German, Swiss, Italian.
Belgium	RTL, German, Dutch, French, British on the coast. All boosted by CATV operators.
Denmark	German in southern third; Swedish and some Norwegian in northern half.
Finland	Swedish, Russian, and Norwegian in the north (STL taken on cable).
France	RTL, Belgian in the north; TMC and Italian in the south; German in the east.
Germany	Border regions only; RTL, French, Belgian, Danish, Austrian, and East German.
Greece	—
Iceland	—
Ireland	British and Northern Irish.
Italy	Border regions only; Swiss, Austrian, TMC, and French.
Luxembourg	Total penetration; Belgian, French, and German.
Netherlands	Belgian, German, French, Danish, British on the coast.
Norway	Swedish, Danish in the south (STL taken on cable).
Portugal	Spanish in border regions.
Spain	French and Portuguese in border regions only.
Sweden	Norwegian, Finnish, Danish in the south.
Switzerland	German, French, Italian (STL taken on cable).
United Kingdom	Irish in Ulster and Wales.

Source: Commission of the European Communities, *Television Without Frontiers: Green Paper on the Establishment of the Common Market for Broadcasting, Especially by Satellite and Cable*, COM (84)300, Annex 2, Final, June 1984.

bourg or into Luxembourg, France, and Belgium? Alternatively, has "Dallas" been re-exported from Luxembourg into France and Belgium? Moreover, is it important in this determination whether the Luxembourg broadcaster has sold advertising time based on the combined audience in all three countries? Problems such as this inevitably produce some ambiguity in the data. With the emergence of services trade issues onto the world stage, better data on television programming flows will be gathered and compiled of necessity.

As with films, the most comprehensive data on international flows of television programs are found in UNESCO surveys. Surveys conducted by Tapio Varis in 1973 and 1983 (the first with Kaarle Nordenstreng) are of particular interest.[3] As with the UNESCO surveys on films, the Varis and Varis and Nordenstreng surveys measure only one dimension of trade; in this case, hours of programs. However, the basic trade patterns that stand out in the program hours data also appear to be reflected in available data on audiences and financial flows. In addition, the Varis and Varis and Nordenstreng surveys show that while exchanges of programming within regional trading groups became more important between the surveys, the most important structural feature of the global programming trade—domination of program supply by a few major exporting nations—did not change.

The United States is by far the largest supplier of imported television programming, as well as films, in most areas of the world. The Varis and Nordenstreng study reported that during the early 1970s the United States exported approximately 150,000 hours of programming each year. This was more than three times the total programming exports of the next three leading exporting nations combined (the United Kingdom, France, and West Germany). The United States was the source of about 75 percent of the programming imported into Latin America and 44 percent of that into Western Europe.[4] In addition, the United States, along with the United Kingdom, was the main supplier of imported programming into Asia, the Middle East, and the Republic of South Africa. Like the United States, the other countries identified as major suppliers of imported programming (the United Kingdom, France, West Germany, and Japan) are also among the nations listed by UNESCO as major international suppliers of films.

The parallel between trade in films and trade in television programming extends to American imports. Imports account for only a small fraction of the programs shown on American television. In Varis's 1973 and 1983 surveys, the United States imported between 1 and 2 percent of its total television programming. By contrast, imported programs accounted for approximately one-third or more of total programming time in other countries (see Table 3–3).

While the scarcity of imported programming in the United States (identified in the UNESCO survey) is significant, the relatively low levels of imports mask an important recent phenomenon, namely, the rise of foreign-produced Spanish-language programming on U.S. cable systems andSpanish tele-vision stations. The Spanish International Network (SIN), now Univision, has supplied imported programming from Mexico to U.S. cable systems and broadcast affiliates throughout the country since 1967. SIN obtained its Spanish-language program-ming from its parent, Televisa, the privately owned Mexican broadcast system. As of 1983, SIN could reach 90 percent of the Latin people living in the United States through its nearly two hundred U.S. affiliates.[5] In 1982 it had advertising revenues of $35 million and was called the fourth-largest commercial net-work in the United States.[6] (The significance of SIN as an importer of Spanish-language programming into the United States is discussed further in Chapter 5.)

The UNESCO surveys and other sources indicate the exis-tence of distinct regional trading areas with their own important suppliers in addition to the countries identified as major global producers. Important regional suppliers include Brazil and Mex-ico in Latin America, Egypt in the Arab world, Hong Kong in Southeast Asia, and the Soviet Union in Eastern Europe. In Western Europe, such regional television exchanges as Eurovi-sion contribute to intraregional program flows. The data also suggest that the Eastern European nations constitute something of a closed trading block in that these countries buy and sell programs from each other but trade very little with other nations.

Unfortunately, little data exist on the audiences generated by imported programs. The limited information on television audiences suggests that the fraction of broadcast hours devoted to imported programs is larger than the fraction of a nation's audience that watches the imports, at least in countries that have significant domestic production industries. A recent study of programming trends in Brazil, for example, demonstrated that, over time, increases in broadcast hours devoted to imported

Table 3–3. Percentage of Imported Television Programs in 1973 and 1983.

Region, Country, and Broadcasting Institution	Percentage of Programming Imported	
	1973	1983
North America		
Canada/CBC	34	32
Canada/RC	46	38
United States/commercial	1	2
United States/educational	2	
Latin America and Caribbean		
Argentina/Canal 9	10	49
Brazil	—	30
Chile	55	—
Colombia	34	—
Cuba	—	24
Dominican Republic	50	—
Ecuador	—	66
Guatemala	84	—
Mexico	39	34
Uruguay	62	—
Venezuela	—	38
Western Europe		
Austria	—	43
Belgium/BRT	—	28
Belgium/RTBF	—	29
Denmark	—	46
Federal Republic of Germany/ARD	23	13
Federal Republic of Germany/ZDF	30	23
Federal Republic of Germany/Regional	—	24
Finland	40	37
France	9	17
Greece	—	39
Iceland	67	66
Ireland	54	57
Italy	13	18
Netherlands	23	25
Norway	39	30
Portugal	35	39
Spain	—	33
Spain/EIT. B Regional	—	74

Table 3–3 continued.

Region, Country, and Broadcasting Institution	Percentage of Programming Imported	
	1973	1983
Sweden	33	35
Turkey	—	36
United Kingdom/BBC	12	15
United Kingdom/ITV	13	14
United Kingdom/Channel 4	—	26
Eastern Europe/Soviet Union		
Bulgaria	47	27
German Democratic Republic	26	30
Czechoslovakia	—	24
Hungary	24	26
Poland	17	—
Romania	27	—
Soviet Union	5	8
Yugoslavia	27	29
Asia and the Pacific		
Australia	57	44
Brunei	—	60
People's Republic of China	1	8
Hong Kong/Asia TV Chinese	31	24
Hong Kong/Asia TV English	40	64
Hong Kong/Asia TV Ltd.	—	27
India/Calcutta	—	3
India/Delhi	—	11
Japan/NHK educational	1	—
Japan/commercial	10	—
Republic of Korea/Tong-yang	31	—
Republic of Korea/Munhwa TV	—	16
Malaysia	71	54
New Zealand/one	75	72
New Zealand/two	75	75
Pakistan	35	16
Philippines	29	12
Philippines/Metro Manila	—	40
Singapore/Channel 8	78	55
Singapore/Channel 5	78	70
Sri Lanka	—	24

Table 3–3 continued.

Region, Country, and Broadcasting Institution	Percentage of Programming Imported	
	1973	1983
Thailand	18	—
Vietnam	—	34
Near East and Arab Countries		
Algeria	—	55
Egypt	41	35
Israel	55	—
Kuwait	56	—
Lebanon	40	—
Saudi-Arabia/Aramco TV	100	—
Syria	—	33
Tunisia	—	55
People's Republic of Yemen	57	47
Africa		
Ghana	27	—
Kenya	—	37
Nigeria	63	40
Republic of South Africa	—	29
Uganda	19	38
Zambia	64	—
Zimbabwe	—	61

Source: Tapio Varis, "The International Flow of Television Programs," *Journal of Communication* 34, no. 1, 1984: 143–75 ©1984 *Journal of Communication*. Reprinted by permission.

television far surpassed the growth in *audience hours* that could be attributed to the same imported product.[7] This anomaly seemingly resulted from programming decisions by Brazilian broadcasters who began to substitute Brazilian programming for U.S. fare during prime time. However, Brazilian broadcasters were simultaneously purchasing more American programs for use in daytime and late-night spots where the smaller audiences could not support Brazilian-produced programs. It is almost certain that measures of broadcast hours also overstate audiences generated by U.S. programs relative to domestic productions in Mexico and Japan, and probably in many other countries as well.[8]

Data on the financial magnitude of trade in television programming are extremely limited. United States producers earned about $500 million in 1984 from the sale of television programming in foreign markets.[9] An estimate of the growth in foreign television sales achieved by members of the Motion Picture Export Association of America (MPEAA) is provided in Table 3–4.

Table 3–4. Growth in Foreign Television Program Syndication Revenues (MPEAA members).

Year	$U.S. Millions
1963	66
1964	70
1965	73
1966	70
1967	78
1968	80
1969	99
1970	97
1971	85
1972	90
1973	127
1974	150
1975	175
1976	180
1977	210
1978	230
1979	281
1980	320
1981	361
1982	421
1983	485

Source: Jean Luc Renaud and Barry R. Litman, "Changing Dynamics of the Overseas Market Place for TV Programming," *Telecommunications Policy* 9, no. 3 (September 1985): 249. (Reprinted with permission.)

TYPES OF PROGRAMS TRADED

Entertainment programs comprise most of imported television programming (see Table 3–5). They constitute 71 percent of imported programs in Latin America, but only 44 percent of total programming in that region; in Western Europe, they account for 53 percent of imported programs, but only 35 percent of total programming. Relative to their share of total programming, imports are a significant source of sports programming in many nations.

While motion pictures shown on television are important American exports (see Table 3–6 for the origin of films shown on television in Europe), dramatic and comedy series also contribute heavily to the U.S. export total. American television executives have recently begun to express interest in exporting other types of programming into foreign markets. For example, NBC has announced plans to supply news programming to cable television systems and hotels in Western Europe.[10] Cable News Network's (CNN) Ted Turner already provides news programming in Western Europe, primarily to hotels. In addition, U.S. sports programmers have begun to test entry into the international market, as is evidenced by recent broadcasts of American-style football to British audiences.

For non-U.S. exporters of television programming, particularly those in Latin American countries, the entertainment category is also important. Both Brazil and Mexico export *telenovelas*, a particular type of dramatic series that is popular with Spanish- and Portugese-speaking audiences. For the four Latin American countries of Mexico, Brazil, Venezuela, and Argentina, *telenovelas* account for 70 percent of total exports.[11] Comedy shows (18 percent) and musicals and variety programs (12 percent) constitute the balance of exported programming.[12] Approximately 65 percent of the programming shown on SIN consists of *telenovelas* and variety shows originally broadcast by Televisa. SIN also broadcasts *telenovelas* from Spain, Argentina, Puerto Rico, and Venezuela.[13]

Table 3–5. Distribution of Programs by Region and Category (percent).

Category	United States		Canada		Latin America		Western Europe	
	All	Imports	All	Imports	All	Imports	All	Imports
Informative	19	1	35	—	16	20	29	5
Educational	7	0	8	—	7	13	9	10
Cultural	6	9	8	24	2	14	6	12
Religious	3	—	2	28	1	18	1	11
Entertainment	40	2	36	72	44	71	35	53
Sports	4	2	3	—	5	18	8	36
Other (advertisements, children's, etc.)	25	0	8	35	25	37	12	30
Total %	100		100		100		100	
Total minutes	17,344,100		84,166		670,088		236,207	

Source: Tapio Varis, "The International Flow of Television Programs," *Journal of Communication* 34, no. 1 (1984): 143–75 © 1984 *Journal of Communication*. Reprinted by permission.

Table 3–6. European Economic Community: Origin of Films Shown on Television in 1981.

| | Country of Origin | | | | | | | | | | | | |
| | Belgium | | France | | Germany | | Italy | | United Kingdom | | United States | | Other | |
Country of Showing	No.	%	No.	%	No.	%	No.	%	No.	%	No.	%	No.	%
Belgium RIBF			160	48.8	15	4.3	24	6.8	12	3.4	107	30.70	17	4.9
BRI			11	6.25	7	3.98	4	2.28	24	13.64	104	59.10	26	14.17
France[a]	—	—			4	2.29	8	4.59	12	6.89	140	80.45	10	5.74
Germany[b]	—	—	48	11.79			15	3.68	26	6.38	221	54.29	93	22.85
United Kingdom[c]	—	—	6	1.14	2	0.38	6	1.14			491	93.70	20	3.81

Source: Commission of the European Communities, *Television Without Frontiers: Green Paper on the Establishment of the Common Market for Broadcasting, Especially by Satellite and Cable,* COM(84)300, Annex 3, p. 334, June 1984.

a. TF, FR 3; figures broken down by country of origin not available for A2.

b. ARD, ZDF; the ZDF figures include the first half of 1982; coproductions classified according to the first-named country of origin.

c. BBC only.

THE ROLE OF GOVERNMENTS

Governments play a much larger role in determining trade flows in television programming than they do in films. In motion pictures, we can generally assume that, with the exception of completely state-controlled economies, film purchase decisions will reflect, in large part, the profit motive and commercial incentives. While these decisions may be influenced by state-created restrictions and incentives, the importance of financial considerations is unquestionable. The role of the state in broadcasting in most countries, however, makes the influence of commercial considerations on programming decisions much weaker, or eliminates it altogether.

National broadcast systems can be grouped into three loose classifications that reflect the varying role of governments in broadcasting (see Table 3–7). Systems owned and programmed by the government predominate in Eastern Europe and many Third World countries. Public, nonprofit systems, which are responsible for their own programming, exist in Japan and most of the developed Western democracies and are common in Latin America. Historically these have been the only systems permitted by law in most of Western Europe. There are significant differences

Table 3–7. Ownership of Television Broadcasting Systems: Global Summary, 1983.[a]

Type of Ownership	Number	Percent
Government	36	50.7
Public Corporation	26	36.6
Commercial, private	4	5.7
Combinations of the above		
Public/commercial	2	2.8
Government/public/commercial	2	2.8
Government/commercial	1	1.4

Source: UNESCO, *Statistical Yearbook*, 1985 (Paris: UNESCO, 1985), Table 10–7.

a. This UNESCO data series excludes a number of important countries including the United States, which is a mixed public and commercial system.

among public systems in terms of financing—various combinations of government grants, receiver fees, and advertising are employed (see Table 3–8). Finally, a number of countries are similar to the United States in that private commercial broadcast systems are permitted. Private, commercial systems can be found in the United States, most Latin American countries, Canada, the United Kingdom, Australia, Luxembourg, Italy, and Japan. Most countries that permit private, commercial broadcasting simultaneously support some form of public television system.[14]

The absence of overriding commercial motivations for public, noncommercial, and government-controlled broadcast entities has implications for trade in television programming. Noncommercial considerations are reflected in programming decisions. They are also frequently used as justification for the many forms of nontariff barriers to the purchase of foreign programs for domestic viewing. In addition, government policies often reduce the value of domestic program markets, both to program exporters and to domestic producers. This also affects trade in programming. We return to these issues in Chapter 5.

Governments' influence in international trade in television is extended, at least indirectly, through the International Telecommunications Union (ITU). The ITU is an agency of the United Nations and acts as the technical regulator for international telecommunications and broadcast activities.[15] Through such working groups as the International Frequency Registration Board, the ITU monitors worldwide use of specific frequencies within the electromagnetic spectrum. In addition, through various worldwide technical conferences, it periodically reviews communications regulations and makes decisions as to the allocation of frequency bands to alternate or emergency communications uses. The 1983 North American Regional Conference on DBS (Direct Broadcast Satellite) allotments, which allocated orbital slots among countries, is one example of how such groups function. In this instance, the potential to affect trade flows is obvious as these decisions effectively determine the satellite capacity that can be allocated to commercial uses, including international transmission of television programming. The demand of the Third World nations at the World Adminis-

Table 3–8. Annual Radio and Television License Fees per Household in EEC Countries, 1983 (in national currency).[a]

	Radio	Television		Combined Fee	
		Black/White	Color	Black/White	Color
Belgium BFR	708 ($12.73)	—	2,688 ($48.35)	4,200[b] ($75.54)	3,625[b] ($65.20)
Denmark DKR	154 (15.59)	—	640 (64.78)	1,080 (109.31)	—
Germany DM	67 (24.63)	—	134 (49.26)	195 (71.69)	—
France FF	311 (37.35)	471 ($56.41)	—	—	—
Greece DR	[c]	[c]	[c]	[c]	[c]
Ireland IRL	—	27 (30.65)	45 (51.08)	—	—
Italy LIT	3,630 (2.19)	—	—	42,680 (25.71)	78,910 (47.54)
Luxembourg LFR	[d]	[d]	[d]	[d]	[d]
Netherlands HFL	45 (14.71)	—	—	—	153 (50.00)
United Kingdom UKL	—	15 (21.77)	46 (66.76)	—	—

Source: European Economic Community, *Television Without Frontiers*, Green Paper on the Establishment of the Common Market for Broadcasting, Especially by Satellites and Cable, June 14, 1984, Annex 6.

a. $U.S. 1983 equivalent in parentheses.

b. Average combined fee for cable, radio, and television.

c. No license fee, but extra charge included on electricity bill.

d. No license fee.

trative Radio Conference (WARC '79) that some satellite orbital slots be left unoccupied for their eventual use illustrates the political tug of war that ultimately determines spectrum allocations at ITU conferences.

SATELLITE DISTRIBUTION OF TELEVISION PROGRAMS

Since the International Telecommunications Satellite Organization (INTELSAT) achieved "global" signal coverage with the successful operation of satellites over the Atlantic, Pacific, and Indian Oceans in 1969, the importance of satellite distribution of television programming has increased dramatically. In 1970, INTELSAT carried slightly more than 1,000 hours of television programming. By 1980, its programming volume had increased nearly tenfold.[16] A recent study has placed the *transatlantic* flow of television programs at approximately 20,000–30,000 hours for 1985.[17]

The INTELSAT consortium offers satellite services to 109 member nations around the world.[18] In addition, nonmember nations can purchase satellite time, bringing the total number of countries with access to INTELSAT to 170.[19] Each nation maintains one or more earth stations that allow access to all other participating nations via satellite interconnection.

Several groups of nations have also joined to provide regional satellite associations. ARABSAT, a consortium of twenty-two Middle East and North African countries, has proposed a pan-Arab television broadcast service. Five Scandinavian nations have discussed a regional system, the satellite, to be called NORDSAT.[20] In Europe, the European Space Agency (ESA) launched the satellite ECS-1 in 1983.[21] On ECS-1, nine transponders have been allocated among West Germany, the United Kingdom, Belgium, France, Italy, the Netherlands, Norway, and Sweden.

Broadcast satellites are used to transmit television programs in several different ways. Signals may be transmitted from:

Satellite to broadcaster;

Satellite to broadcaster to cable system;

Satellite to cable system;

Satellite to PAY TV (subscriber-supported television) or SMATV (Satellite Master Antennae Television) systems;[22]

Satellite to theater; or

Satellite to home.

Satellites may deliver signals directly to the subscriber's home, if the home is equipped with a home-reception antenna. A significant audience for this form of direct broadcast has failed to develop in most nations as satellite reception antennae are very expensive. However, if antennae sizes (and cost) could be reduced dramatically, satellite-to-home service would become widespread. Proponents of DBS program services justify such systems on these grounds.

In order to communicate with very small reception antennae, DBS satellites must be capable of transmitting powerful signals. Accordingly, such satellites are very costly, ranging from four to six times the cost of conventional broadcast satellites.[23] Despite the magnitude of these expenditures, DBS systems are moving toward implementation, particularly in Europe. As of March 1986, TVSAT, the West German DBS satellite, was scheduled to be launched in late 1986, while the French DBS vehicle, TDF-1, had a planned launch date in the fall of 1987.[24]

CABLE TELEVISION

The emergence of satellite distribution has provided the technological impetus to expand cable distribution facilities in the United States and in certain other high-income countries. European nations, the Benelux countries in particular, have wired many of their households for cable reception, although the number of wired households differs widely across nations[25] (see

Table 3–9). Current estimates suggest that about 10 million of Europe's 125 million television households are now wired for cable, approximately two-thirds of which are in the countries of Belgium, the Netherlands, and Switzerland.[26]

The opportunity to link satellite and cable technology for the provision of satellite-delivered programming in Europe has attracted a number of entrants into this market, the largest being Rupert Murdoch's Sky Channel (see Table 3–10). The impact that these entrants have had on the regulated European television industry has been profound. Satellite "footprints" do not conform to national borders. For this reason, control of signal reception by national authorities is more complicated than the regulation of terrestrially dependent broadcasters. Signal overspill, even when programming is received by means of conventional cross-border broadcast or cable retransmission, undermines traditional national sovereignty over television.

Loss of national control threatens established practices in several ways. For one, advertising regulations can no longer be tailored to the cultural sensitivities of individual nations. Accordingly, national regulations cannot set quantitative advertis-

Table 3–9. European Households Wired to Cable Systems and Master Antennae, 1984.

Country	Cable Systems	Master Antennae Systems
Belgium	1,700,000	—
Denmark	NA	1,000,000
Germany	NA	9,700,000
France	400,000	6–8,000,000
Ireland	200,000	—
Luxembourg	60,000	—
Netherlands	2,800,000[a]	—
United Kingdom	2,600,000	—

Source: European Economic Community, *Television Without Frontiers, Green Paper on the Establishment of the Common Market for Broadcasting, Especially by Satellites and Cable,* June 14, 1984, pp. 18, 19.

a. Includes community antennae households.

ing limits or commercial content rules without considering the views of neighboring countries.[27] Similarly, copyright protection, particularly the control of exclusive distribution in national markets, now faces increased difficulties in implementation. The EEC has attempted to address many of these issues in its various reports on pan-European television. We discuss the EEC's specific proposals to expand transborder television later in this book.

Table 3–10. European Cable Television.

Channel	Base	Owners	Delivery	Ad-Supported/ Pay TV	Content	Homes
Arts Channel	Britain	W.H. Smith (31%) Television South (11%) Commercial Union (11%) Equity and Law (11%)	Intelsat VA-FII	Ad-supported	Culture and arts	6,000
Bravo	Britain	Cablevision U.K.	Videotape	Ad-supported	Classic films	1,000
Cable News Network	United States	Turner Broadcasting	Intelsat VA-FII		News	—
Children's Channel	Britain	Thom EMI (33.3%) British Telecom (33.3%) D.C. Thomson (33.3%)	Intelsat VA-FII	Ad-supported	Kidvid	91,000
Europa TV	Holland	ARD (West Germany) NOS (Holland) RAI (Italy) RTE (Ireland) RTP (Portugal)	Eutelsat I-FI	Ad-supported	General	1,300,000
Filmnet	Holland	Esselte/UDF (40%) UIP (20%) VNU (20%)	Eutelsat I-FI	Pay TV	Films	65,000
Home Video Channel	Britain	British Telecom	Videotape	Ad-supported	Films	1,000
Janco-Vision	Norway	Orkla Industries	Videotape	Pay TV	General	140,000
Lifestyle	Britain	W.H. Smith (40%) Television South (20%) Yorkshire TV (20%) D.C. Thomson (20%)	Intelsat VA-FII	Ad-supported	Daytime	40,000

Name	Country	Shareholders	Satellite	Type	Genre	Subscribers
Music Box	Britain	Virgin (60%), Yorkshire TV (20%), Granada TV (20%)	Eutelsat I-FI	Ad-supported	Pop music	3,900,000
Musicbox	West Germany	KMP, Munich	Intelsat V-FI	Ad-supported	Pop music	439,000
New World	Norway	ARD	Eutelsat I-FI	Ad-supported	Religious	83,000
1-Plus	West Germany	SRG (Switzerland)	Intelsat V-FI		General	430,000
Premiere	Britain	Mirror Group (51%), Columbia (12.25%), Twentieth Century Fox (12.25%), Home Box Office (12.25%), Showtime/TMC (12.25%)	Intelsat VA-FII	Pay TV	Films	46,000
RAI	Italy	RAI	Eutelsat I-FI	Ad-supported	General	1,444,000
RTL-Plus	Luxembourg	CLT (60%), Bertelsmann (40%)	Eutelsat I-FI	Ad-supported	General	1,450,000
SAT-1	West Germany	PKS, APF, Springer, Burda, Bauer, KMP, Frankfurter Allgemeine, Neue Medien, Ravensburger Film OMV	Eutelsat I-FI	Ad-supported	General	1,153,000
Screen Sport	Britain	W.H. Smith, ESPN, ABC, RCA, 3i	Intelsat VA-FII	Ad-supported (+ pay TV outside United Kingdom)	Sports	125,000

Table 3–10 continued.

Channel	Base	Owners	Delivery	Ad-Supported/ Pay TV	Content	Homes
Sky Channel	Britain	News Intl. (83%) Ferranti Ladbroke D.C. Thomson Equity and Law	Eutelsat I-FI	Ad-supported	General	5,800,000
Teleclub	Switzerland	Rediffusion AG (60%) Beta-Taurus (40%)	Eutelsat I-FI	Pay TV	Films	20,500
3-Sat	West Germany	ZDF ORD SRG	Eutelsat I-FI	Ad-supported	General	1,450,000
TV-5	France	TF-1 A-2 (80%) FR-3 RTBF, Belgium (14.4%) SSR, Switzerland (14.4%) Radio Canada	Eutelsat I-FI		General	3,500,000
Viidekanava	Finland	Helsinki Televisio	Videotape	Pay TV	Films/Series	23,000
Worldnet	United States	U.S. Information Agency	Eutelsat I-FI		Information	815,000
World Public News	Belgium	International Television Services	Eutelsat I-FI	Sponsored	Information	636,000

Source: "European Cable Television Chart," *Variety,* April 23, 1986, p. 46.

NOTES

1. Tapio Varis, "The International Flow of Television Programs," *Journal of Communications* 34, no. 1 (Winter 1984): 143.
2. *Official Report of the Games of the XXIIIrd Olympiad* (Los Angeles: Los Angeles Olympic Organizing Committee, 1984), vol. 1, p. 764.
3. Tapio Varis and Kaarle Nordenstreng, "Television Traffic, A One-Way Street," (Paris: Boudin/UNESCO, 1974) and Varis, "The International Flow of Television Programs."
4. Varis and Nordenstreng, "Television Traffic," p. 274.
5. Felix F. Gutierrez and Jorge Reina Schement, "Spanish International Network: The Flow of Television From Mexico to the United States," *Communications Research* 11, no. 2 (April 1984): 251.
6. Ibid., p. 253.
7. Joseph Straubhaar, "Brazilian Television: The Decline of American Influence," *Communications Research* 11, no. 2 (April 1984): 230–31.
8. Richard Gertner, ed., *1986 International Television Almanac,* 31st ed., (New York: Quigley Publishing Company, 1986), p. 650.
9. "Global Prices for TV Films," *Variety,* April 23, 1986, p. 58.
10. John Lippman, "NBC Tackles Euro Cable Market," *Variety,* October 1, 1986, p.1.
11. Livia Antola and Everett M. Rogers, "Television Flows in Latin America," *Communications Research* 11, no. 2 (April 1984): 187.
12. Ibid.
13. Ibid., p. 195.
14. The commercial/public system mix is currently in flux in most EEC countries. There is strong support for introducing commercial broadcasting in most community nations, and some governments, such as that in France, have already begun licensing commercial broadcasters.
15. The ITV follows the UN principle of equal voting rights for each member nation.
16. Sydney W. Head, *World Broadcasting Systems* (Belmont; Calif.: Wadsworth Publishing Company, 1985), p. 37.
17. U.S. Congress, Office of Technology Assessment, *Intellectual Property Rights in an Age of Electronics and Information,* OTA-CIT-302 (Washington, D.C.: April 1986), p. 221. Original

source, Kalba Bowen Associates Inc., *The Economist Connections: World Communications Reports*, no. 32, May 24, 1985, p. 8.

18. Head, *World Broadcasting Systems*, p. 37.
19. Ibid.
20. Ibid., p. 43.
21. Ibid., p. 44.
22. One form of PAY TV is Subscription TV (STV), whereby a scrambled over-the-air signal may be received by audiences paying a subscription fee. SMATV provides for the connection of up to 300 subscribers to a common antenna in a single housing complex that receives programming via satellite.
23. Annual transponder costs on Europe's conventional satellite ECS-1 range between $1.2 and $2.3 million. DBS transponder charges are expected to fall between $8.2 and $16.4 million. See "TV Satellites Fill Up European Skies: Detailed Look at a New Era," *Variety*, August 22, 1984, p. 79.
24. "The Privatization of Europe" *Broadcasting* 110, no. 13 (March 31, 1986): 63.
25. The estimation of cable-wired households in Europe is complicated by the presence of numerous master antennae and community antennae systems that carry far fewer channels than coaxial cable-based systems common in the United States.
26. "The Privatization of Europe," p. 61.
27. Indeed, stringent limits on the amount of advertising that can be shown by European public broadcasters almost certainly increased demand for new advertising vehicles such as Sky Channel. See Brenda Maddox, "Sky King," *Channels of Communication* 5, no. 5. (January/February 1986): 55.

4

AN ECONOMIC MODEL OF TRADE IN VIDEO PRODUCTS

As we saw in Chapters 2 and 3, American film makers and television producers realize substantial revenues from rentals and sales of their products in foreign markets. This contrasts with the revenues generated by films and television programs imported from other nations into the United States, which are quite small by comparison. This disparity reflects the fact that, while most Americans rarely watch foreign films and television programs, American video productions draw large audiences in other countries. In this chapter we introduce an economic model of trade in video products that explains the prominence of American products in the world markets for films and television programming. An understanding of the intuition behind this model is essential to the discussion of the effects of trade barriers in Chapter 7 as well as the policy prescriptions presented in Chapter 9.

We are by no means the first to try to explain the fact that U.S. productions dominate international flows of films and television programs. However, the model of trade in video products developed in this chapter and Appendix B is, to our knowledge, the first systematic application of the tools of microeconomic analysis to the subject of patterns of trade in video products. Furthermore, because the model is developed in general terms, it is useful for the study of trade flows of video products in general and the cases of the American film and television program industry in particular. Much of the earlier work on video trade flows focused more· narrowly on the characteristics of the U.S. video industries. Chapter 5 shows that the global patterns of trade in video products documented in Chapters 2 and 3 are consistent with the model developed here.

Before presenting our model of international trade in video products, we discuss briefly earlier analyses and what we perceive as their shortcomings.[1]

PREVIOUS ANALYSES OF TRADE IN VIDEO PRODUCTS

The term "free flow" is associated both with an earlier economic explanation of trade flows in media products and with the political doctrine concerning trade in media products that was dominant in international political bodies (most importantly, in the United Nations) in the decades immediately following World War II. The assumption underlying the free flow political doctrine was that the unhindered transmission of information across national borders was mutually beneficial to all parties. Within this paradigm, the mass media, especially television, were seen as vehicles that facilitated the flow of information. The economic argument implicit in the free flow doctrine was articulated later when it became clear that the products of American media firms dominated this flow. Trade patterns in media products, it was argued, were a consequence of market forces. In particular, the large share of the trade in media products accounted for by U.S. corporations was a consequence of the more sophisticated technology employed by American firms that enabled them to produce films and television programs at lower cost than foreign competitors could. According to the theory of comparative advantage, both parties to a trade benefit when they each export products in which they have a cost advantage.[2]

As an explanation for media trade flows, the American hegemony paradigm was developed later and in opposition to the free flow position. *Mass Communications and American Empire* by Herbert Schiller (1969) is the best known early statement of the American hegemony paradigm.[3] According to advocates of this paradigm, market forces alone are not sufficient to account for the dominant position of American media products, especially television programs, in Third World nations. Whether by direct "conspiracy" or through a recognition of mutual interests,

American multinational corporations are alleged to control media trade flows so as to assure that American product dominates. American domination of trade in media products, in turn, is complementary to the foreign policy objectives of the United States government. From the hegemony perspective, American media products, including films and, more importantly, television programs, are tools employed by the U.S. government and U.S. multinationals to influence public opinion in other countries and to promote American values and products in Third World nations. The hegemony paradigm gained increasing acceptance within the United Nations during the early 1970s. UNESCO's mass media activities and pronouncements reflecting this perspective were also a factor in the recent U.S. decision to withdraw funding from UNESCO.

A third explanation advanced to explain the importance of American films and television programs in other countries is that American firms employ "unfair" or anticompetitive methods to achieve their market positions. This charge arises most often with regard to films, where it is alleged that American firms employ their positions as major distributors to provide favorable treatment for American films and to discriminate against foreign films of equivalent artistic and commercial merit. This argument is voiced most frequently in trade proceedings and in the reports of government-appointed commissions investigating the competitiveness of indigenous film and television production industries.[4] Of course, the unfair competition argument is not incompatible with the American hegemony paradigm.

What might be called an "affordability" explanation for the success of American video products may be found in scattered statements by officials of production companies based outside the United States and by representatives of trade associations for video industries in other countries. The affordability explanation also surfaces occasionally in politically commissioned reports on the film and television industries in various countries. It attributes at least a part of the success of U.S. video products in international markets to the fact that U.S. firms generally commit more resources to production than do video producers in other countries. This difference in budgets also helps explain the fact that films and television programs from most other countries rarely succeed in the U.S. market.[5] Production budgets are larger in America because the large U.S. market makes large budget productions affordable.

Close examination of the data on trade in video products and a thorough analysis of the economics of video industries reveal serious deficiencies in each of the explanations for observed patterns of trade in video products. The fact that trade in video products between the United States and other developed nations exhibits the same, nearly unidirectional character as that of trade in video products between the United States and less developed nations is a problem for both the free flow and the American hegemony paradigms. The free flow explanation of trade patterns in films and television programs assumes that video products will flow from technologically advanced to less technologically advanced nations. While differences in technological sophistication and patterns of video trade between the United States and Third World nations are consistent with the free flow explanation, it is not plausible to argue that differences in technological capabilities account for U.S. dominance of the video trade between it and the advanced economies of Western Europe and Japan. Furthermore, the production technology and know-how required to produce high-quality motion pictures and television programs is very mobile and exportable. American producers frequently produce on-location films and television programs with stories set in countries besides the United States. In fact, the movement towards production in locations outside the United States has become so large that concerns have arisen in Hollywood about "runaway production." Because the technology employed in producing video products is a matter of choice to firms and is not exogenously determined, differences in technological sophistication cannot be a satisfying explanation for trade flows.

The fact that the pattern of trade in video products between the United States and other advanced economies is similar to the pattern of trade between it and less economically advanced nations is also difficult to explain within the hegemony paradigm. It is hard to believe that the other industrialized nations, whose policies are obviously independent of and frequently at odds with those of the United States in other, more important arenas (e.g., French participation in NATO, German and Japanese policies on interest rates), cannot muster the political muscle required to enforce policies for video industries that would be in their own best interests. Furthermore, as is pointed out by Schement et al.,[6] the existence of reverse flows of programs from Third World nations to the United States, as in the case of SIN,[1] is inconsistent with the hegemony paradigm.

Anticompetitive acts by American distribution companies do not constitute a convincing explanation for the success of American productions; it is clear that American video products enjoy similar degrees of success in markets where the anticompetitive practices hypothesis is obviously not tenable. The charge of unfair competition is heard most often with regard to films, where the commercial context is one in which the domestic distribution arm of an American film company deals with private, domestically owned theaters. That requirements imposed by distributors on exhibitors make the showing of domestically produced films unprofitable is the most frequent charge. However, American films are extremely successful in countries where American producers are allowed to set up their own distribution arms (as in most Western European nations and Japan) and in countries where they are required to rely on domestic distributors (such as South Korea and Iraq). Furthermore, as was shown in Chapter 3, American productions enjoy success in television that parallels that of American films in most nations. Broadcasting systems in most nations are nationalized[7] and can follow purchasing policies that are independent of narrow commercial motivations.[8] Government broadcasting systems are monopsony buyers of television programming. Therefore, if any party is able to exert market power anticompetitively, it would be the government purchasers.[9] The popularity of American films in countries that require the use of domestic distributors and the numbers of American productions on state-owned television systems both suggest that the contribution of anticompetitive practices to the success of American films and television programs in foreign markets is marginal at best.[10]

The affordability explanation is not a model of trade at all, since a causal link between the large U.S. domestic market and larger budgets for U.S. film and television productions is not articulated. One could just as easily assert that the size of the U.S. market should lead to the production of expensive automobiles, such as Mercedes and Rolls Royce, by U.S. firms. While it is true that, other things equal, the greater aggregate purchasing power of consumers *could* make possible the financing of more expensive commodities and services (if consumers pooled their resources) in large rather than small markets, there is no reason why this should be an outcome generated by market forces; moreover, such an explanation says nothing about *where* more expensive products and services will be produced.

It is likely that the affordability explanation is based on an unarticulated intuition that is close to the model of trade presented in the remainder of this chapter. In the following sections, we present a model that shows that under certain conditions, larger markets do lead to greater expenditures on products, such as films and television programs, for which the public good component is large.[11] However, it is not the markets that are defined by political boundaries that are important to this relationship so much as it is the markets that are defined by linguistic and cultural similarities and differences. The model developed in this chapter, in combination with the information on different linguistic markets presented in the next chapter, strongly suggests that the incentives provided by a populous and wealthy global English-language market are responsible for the fact that American products loom so large in the international trade in films and television programs. More generally, the model predicts, and the evidence supports, a strong, positive relationship between the importance of trade in films and television programs produced in any language and the total purchasing power of native speakers of that language. Films from Third World nations and most small countries generally enjoy only limited international success because the expenditures on video entertainment by the speakers of the languages of these countries are small compared to expenditures on video entertainment in countries whose citizens belong to major linguistic groups.

THE MODEL

Assumptions

In spite of the rather extensive literature on trade in video products, and media products in general, that has proliferated over the last forty years, a systematic description of the structural conditions that must be satisfied if trade is to occur had not been offered until fairly recently. In their perceptive article on the subject, Schement et al. list four structural requirements for trade in television programming.[12] Analogous conditions would have to be satisfied for trade in any media products. The Schement et al. conditions are stated here in their general form. First, there must exist within the receiving country a target audience that can be linguistically matched to video products produced in the exporting country. The target audience may speak the language in which the video products of the exporting country are produced, or matching may occur through translation (as by dubbing or subtitling). Second, the target audience must possess the technological means to receive the video products intended for it. For example, in the early days of Spanish programming in the United States, viewers needed UHF converters in order to receive Spanish-language programs.[13] Third, the importing country must provide financial support for the video products. This could be in the form of advertiser payments for commercial time during imported programs in the case of commercial broadcast television or payments by the government or public agencies for programming on noncommercial broadcast systems. For films and videocassettes, financial support generally takes the form of direct viewer payments. Finally, the regulatory/political climate in both the exporting and receiving countries must be favorable to trade. Direct opposition by either national government will inhibit or eliminate trade between them.

The trade model developed in this chapter assumes that these conditions are satisfied. However, Schement et al. focused on the *existence* of bidirectional trade in video products. We focus on the *relative magnitudes* of films and television programming exported by different countries. In extending the analysis to consider the relative magnitudes of trade flows, we employ three additional assumptions. First, we assume that all else held equal, viewers prefer films and television programs in their native languages to films and programs in other languages. Translation, whether performed by the viewer or provided through dubbing and subtitles, diminishes the audience appeal of a film or program. Second, we assume that larger production budgets generally result in films and programming that audiences find more attractive. While pure luck alone may dictate the success of an occasional low-budget film or program, producers can increase the likelihood of creating a popular vehicle by spending more on the inputs that contribute to audience appeal. This can be attained by hiring better writers and directors, employing more popular actors, and spending more money for special effects. Finally, we assume initially that both production and consumption decisions are made in a market setting. This implies profit maximization for producers. We later relax the assumption of a market context.

Granted these assumptions, the model shows that producers in larger countries, and producers in countries that belong to large natural-language markets, have a financial incentive to create larger budget films and programs that will generally have greater intrinsic audience appeal, a clear advantage in international competition. We refer to the market-driven trade advantage that a large linguistic population confers on media products produced in the same language as the domestic opportunity advantage, or DOA. DOAs explain why films and television programs produced in languages with large native-speaking populations dominate the international trade in video entertainment.

Market Size and Production Budgets

Clearly, all other things held constant, the producer's profits are directly proportionate to the audience appeal of the product.

While there is definitely an unpredictable element associated with program popularity, a producer can enhance the expected appeal of a production by spending more money on what we will call the creative inputs of production. For example, popular actors and actresses may contribute substantially to the box office gross or ratings. Better writers are more likely to produce an appealing plot. The quality of directors, choreographers, special effects experts, composers, and musicians also affects the appeal of the final product. Of course, quality comes with a price. In maximizing expected profits, the producer tries to determine the point at which the addition to expected revenue, resulting from an increase in the quality of production inputs, no longer justifies the contribution to expense. Thus one seldom sees major stars playing minor characters. In a minor role, a major star's contribution to revenues would probably not cover the customary salary.

In general, we would expect a profit-seeking producer to spend more on creative inputs the larger the potential market for the film or program. Higher quality inputs should increase the production's share of revenue from the market, and increased share is more valuable in a larger market. Therefore a producer will spend more on inputs before reaching the point at which the increase in expected revenue no longer exceeds the increase in costs. For example, suppose a motion picture producer is competing for audience share in a film market that can be expected to generate $100 million in revenues in a typical year. (This could just as easily be $100 million spent by broadcasters or cable companies on television programming.) Revenue is distributed evenly between producers and exhibitors, assuming, for simplicity, that producers handle distribution. The producers' $50 million is distributed according to audience share. Consider a producer who has a film property that would capture 10 percent of the audience if popular actor A were cast as the lead, but would pull only 5 percent if the less well-known actor B were used instead. Actors A and B charge $5 million and $2 million per picture, respectively. Five percent of $50 million is $2.5 million—

the difference between A's and B's contribution to the producer's revenue. Since A costs $3 million more than B, the producer would contract with B.

Now consider a producer faced with a similar choice between actors in a $200-million market. The revenue to be divided among the producers is $100 million, and the value of the extra 5 percent share of audience contributed by A relative to B is worth $5 million in revenue to the producer. Since A's fee is only $3 million more than B's, the producer would hire A rather than B for a film produced in the larger market. Producers in larger film markets will spend more on higher quality creative inputs in order to increase the audience appeal of their films, holding constant all other things aside from market size.

The other things constant caveat of the preceding sentence demands further consideration. Other producers in the hypothetical market will respond similarly to the same incentives. If all films have greater audience appeal in large markets, it will be more difficult (and more costly) for any individual producer to garner a given share of revenues. The tendency of filmmakers to produce higher budget–higher audience-appeal films in larger markets is therefore self-limiting to some extent. Furthermore, a larger film market may attract more filmmakers. Because filmgoers have diverse tastes, producers are expected to offer an increasingly diverse array of films, thus allowing filmgoers to be more choosy. This fragmentation of the film audience will also make it more difficult for the individual producer to generate box office share, thereby further limiting the tendency to produce films with greater appeal in larger markets.[14] Because consumers value the greater diversity and choice associated with having more films available, as well as the enhanced audience appeal produced by larger budgets, economic intuition suggests that competitive forces will generate both more films and larger budgets in larger markets. The formal economic analysis in Appendix B of a fully specified model of trade in video products supports this intuition. The following example illustrates the logic of that analysis less formally. While the example refers only to films, the conclusions apply equally to television programming.

70

Example

Consider a country in which the portion of the box office gross received by filmmakers is R annually. We are interested in the effects of changes in the magnitude of R on the number of films produced annually, which we indicate by n, and the expenditure on the creative inputs per film that enhance audience appeal, designated by c.

To keep the analysis simple, we assume that filmmakers share in the R of revenue in proportion to their films' audiences and that audience appeal is strictly proportional to the relative expenditure on creative inputs. That is, if filmmaker 1 spends twice as much as does filmmaker 2 on creative inputs, then, on average, filmmaker 1's film would draw twice the audience of filmmaker 2's film; so filmmaker 1's expected share of R would be twice that of filmmaker 2. Total expenditures on creative inputs by all filmmakers in the market are K. If filmmakers 1 and 2 are spending c_1, and c_2 on creative inputs, their shares of the film audience will be c_1/K and c_2/K, and their revenues will be Rc_1/K and Rc_2/K, respectively.

In addition to their expenditures on creative inputs, we assume that filmmakers incur fixed expenses of F as a minimum cost of remaining in the film business. F would include the costs of acquiring and maintaining the minimum equipment required to produce films acceptable for commercial distribution plus salaries of minimum-scale actors and other personnel.

In this simplified film market, all filmmakers perceive the same opportunities and face the same costs for hiring creative inputs. All filmmakers will therefore end up spending the same amount, c, on creative inputs. For n filmmakers, $K = nc$, and each filmmaker can expect revenue of $R(c/K) = R/n$ and realize profits, P, of

$$P = R/n - c - F. \qquad (4.1)$$

In determining a budget for creative inputs, we assume that each filmmaker believes that the size of its production budget does not influence the budget decisions of other filmmakers. Furthermore, we assume that positive profits will induce new filmmakers to enter the industry until each filmmaker is, on average, earning revenues just equal to costs. That is, competition dictates that P equal zero in the long run.

If a filmmaker increases its expenditures on creative inputs, its audience share, and thus film revenue, is increased, but costs are simultaneously increased. The profit-maximizing filmmaker will increase expenditures on creative inputs as long as an additional dollar of expenditure will generate more than a dollar increase in expected revenue. The filmmaker will stop at the point at which a dollar of additional expenditure is just offset by a dollar of additional revenue. It can be shown mathematically that, for the individual filmmaker, setting expenditures on creative inputs at the profit-maximizing level requires that the following relationship must hold in equilibrium.[15]

$$R(n-1)/cn^2 - 1 = 0. \tag{4.2}$$

Equations (1) and (2) can be solved simultaneously to give the following expressions for c and n:

$$c = (RF)^{1/2} - F, \tag{4.3}$$

$$n = (R/F)^{1/2}. \tag{4.4}$$

Equation (3) states that if the total revenue received by filmmakers, R, increases, then the expenditure on creative inputs, c, will also increase, and the increase in c will be proportional to the increase in the square root of R. Equation (4) describes a similar relationship of proportionality between changes in the number of films, n, and changes in R. The importance of Equations (3) and (4) lies not in the specific mathematical relationship shown above, but in the more general relationships they represent— greater expenditures on creative inputs per film and more films produced in markets with larger film revenues. One would expect a market's total film revenue to be positively related to the size and wealth of its population. Therefore, markets with larger and wealthier populations should produce more and better films.[16]

To further illustrate the nature of the relationship between the size of a market and the number and quality of films, consider two countries of different size. Producers in each country make films only for the domestic market. The producers' share of film rentals in Country A is $400 million, while that in Country B is $100 million. Assume that $4 million is the minimum cost for a commercial-quality film.

For Equation (3) we get

$$c_a = \$(400m. \times 4m.)^{1/2} - \$4m = \$36m., \text{ and}$$

$$c_b = \$(100m. \times 4m.)^{1/2} - \$4m = \$16m.$$

as expenditures on creative inputs per film in Countries A and B, respectively. From Equation (4) we get

$$n_a = (400m./4m.)^{1/2} = 10, \text{ and}$$

$$n_b = (100m./4m.)^{1/2} = 5$$

as the numbers of films produced in Countries A and B, respectively. Because the film market in Country A is four times larger than that in Country B, filmgoers in Country A are offered twice as many films as filmgoers in Country B. Furthermore, film budgets in Country A are more than twice as large as those in Country B.

Note that while the number of filmmakers is greater in Country A, it does not increase in proportion to the size of the country. The less than proportional increase in the number of filmmakers reflects the effect that a larger market has on producers' incentives to spend on creative inputs. For a given share of market revenue, a film in Country A will generate four times the revenue of a film in Country B with the identical share. Filmmakers in the larger country thus find it worthwhile to spend more in their attempts to generate share. Because more expensive films are produced in the larger market, the number of films cannot increase in proportion to market revenue. The increased revenue required per film to cover costs limits the increase in the number of films.

Trade among Markets with Different Languages

Two consequences of trade in films (and in television) are immediately apparent from the above example. The total number of films produced by all countries is reduced as the quality of films increases. To continue with the example, suppose that four countries the size of Country B, which previously had purely domestic film industries, decide to open trade in films. Assuming that no language or cultural differences exist to reduce the appeal of one country's films in another, the situation would change from one with four film markets, each with five filmmakers that are producing $16-million films, to one with a single market in which ten filmmakers are each producing $36-million films. The total number of filmmakers would be halved, while expenditure per film would more than double. Consumers would benefit from a doubling in the number of films shown in each country, as well as from an increase in film quality. However, the effect of trade on the number and quality of films and the benefits to consumers will be limited by differences between countries, such as language and culture, that limit the audience appeal of one country's films in another. Therefore the reduction in the four-country total of films and the increase in film expenditures would be less if the language of each country was not perfectly understood by filmgoers in the other countries.[17]

In the above example, equality of size of trading partners masks another important consequence of linguistic differences between countries.[18] (Because linguistic and cultural differences have similar effects on trade in media products, we will refer to the combined effects as linguistic differences only. The analysis, however, applies to cultural differences as well.) In the absence of linguistic differences, one would expect the geographical distribution of film production and the total earnings of each country's filmmakers to approximate the relative sizes of the domestic film markets. This premise is reasonable if a film's reception in the combined market is a function only of relative expenditures on creative inputs. However, if each country has its own language, the fraction of combined film output produced in a large country will be greater than its proportionate contribution to the size of the combined market. In addition, the percentage of total international film rentals going to the films of the larger countries will be greater still.

The disproportionate success of films from large countries when countries differ linguistically is a direct consequence of the previously discussed effect of market size on film quality. In any national market, films that are produced in a foreign language suffer from a handicap that reduces their earnings potential relative to domestically produced films. Small-country filmmakers suffer from the language handicap in a larger portion of the total market than do large-country filmmakers. As a consequence, even with free trade, large-country filmmakers behave as if they are producing films for a larger market. Large-country filmmakers spend more on creative inputs and produce higher quality films. The higher quality of films produced in a large country's language will offset, to some degree, the language handicap that these films encounter in smaller countries. On the other hand, films in small-country languages will face both a language handicap and a quality disadvantage when competing for audiences in larger countries. Thus films in the language of a larger country will be competitively stronger in smaller countries than films in a smaller country's language will be in a large country. As was illustrated above, the market expansion effect of trade in this context implies that fewer filmmakers will serve the international market than if there were no trade in films. Because small-country filmmakers are at a comparative disadvantage in the combined market, their numbers will be affected most. In fact, if the relative difference in the size of large and small countries is large enough, films in the larger countries' languages will be of sufficiently higher quality to eliminate all film production in smaller countries.

The prior example with Countries A and B can be extended to illustrate these points. Assume that the language handicap is such that a $1 expenditure on creative inputs for a Country A film produces the same increase in audience appeal in Country B as does ninety cents spent on a Country B film and vice versa. We know that, without trade, filmmakers in Country A spend $36 million on creative inputs and produce \$40-million films, while Country B filmmakers spend \$16 million on creative inputs for \$20-million films. However, this cannot be an equilibrium if films are traded between A and B. With the no-trade budgets and numbers of filmmakers, filmmakers in Country A will realize profits, once trade is permitted. This will stimulate the development of new filmmakers in Country A. At the same time, filmmakers in Country B will be losing money, and some of the Country B filmmakers will quit the business. This is easy to show.

Let R_{aa} stand for the expected revenue of a Country A film in Country A, and let R_{ab} denote the expected revenue for a Country A film in Country B, given that the numbers of filmmakers and film budgets in the two countries are those given for a no-trade equilibrium above.

$$R_{aa} = (\$400 \; mil) \times (36/(10 \times 36 + .9 \times 5 \times 16)), \; and$$

$$R_{ab} = (\$100 \; mil) \times (.9 \times 36)/(.9 \times 10 \times 36 + 5 \times 16).$$

Similarly, filmmakers from Country B could expect revenues of

$$R_{ba} = (\$400 \; mil) \times (.9 \times 16)/(10 \times 36 + .9 \times 5 \times 16), \; and$$

$$R_{bb} = (\$100 \; mil) \times (16/(.9 \times 10 \times 36 + 5 \times 16))$$

from Countries A and B, respectively.

The sum of R_{aa} and R_{ab} is \$41.35 million while R_{ba} and R_{bb} sum to \$17.29 million. With trade between A and B, each Country A film will earn a profit of \$1.35 million, while each Country B film will lose \$2.71 million, since total costs are \$40 million and \$20 million, respectively. The expectation of positive profits will induce entry by new Country A filmmakers, while some Country B filmmakers will leave the market due to losses.

Filmmakers in both countries have an incentive to increase expenditures on creative inputs. As a result, the cost and quality of films produced in both countries will increase with trade. Using the expressions for R_{aa} and R_{ab}, it is easy to show that if all other filmmakers maintained their production budgets at the no-trade levels, one of the Country A filmmakers could increase its profits to $1.4 million by raising its expenditure on creative inputs to $37 million. Similarly, it can be shown that a Country B filmmaker could reduce its losses to $2.66 million by increasing expenditures on creative inputs to $17 million. Movement toward a new equilibrium with trade between A and B would require entry by new filmmakers in Country A, exit by film-makers in Country B, and higher film budgets in both countries.[19]

MARKETS WITH NONCOMMERCIAL BUYERS

An assumption of the model developed above is that buyers of films or programs (theaters, television stations, networks, etc.) are trying to maximize profits. The commercial box office, which is characteristic of most nonsocialist countries, satisfies this assumption. However, television is a noncommercial enterprise in a collection of national markets that contains a large fraction of the world's television audience. In these countries, broadcast-ing services are provided either by government agencies or by state-chartered noncommercial organizations. Nevertheless, the proposition that larger budget films and television programs will be produced in larger markets should still hold as long as markets with noncommercial broadcast systems are the standard for comparison. Again, this is a consequence of the public good characteristics of films and television programs.

Assuming that the budgets of governments and public agencies are allocated to maximize benefits to constituents, the increase in benefits to the citizenry should be the same for the marginal dollar of expenditure on each item in the budget. That is, the last dollar spent on highways should hold the same value as the last dollar spent on defense, which in turn, should hold the same value as the last dollar spent on television programming, and so on. For a public good, the consumption benefits will increase in proportion to the size of the consuming population. Therefore, if expenditures are increased to the point at which marginal benefits equal marginal costs, there should be greater expenditure on public goods in countries with larger populations. In the case of television programs, this means that if programming is purchased by governments or public agencies, more expensive programming should be purchased, and presumably produced, in larger countries. A wealthier population should have a similar effect on publicly financed program expenditures. Expenditure on entertainment rises with disposable income, therefore a wealthier citizenry should be willing to spend more, in the form of higher taxes, for better (more expensive) programming. Accordingly, even in a world where governments and public agencies are responsible for all television program purchases, we still might observe the pattern of trade in programs, documented in Chapter 3, where programs generally flow from larger and wealthier nations to smaller and poorer ones.

From a purely analytical perspective, there is no necessary relationship between government or public agency control of program purchases and video products trade flows in a world that is populated by both commercial and noncommercial broadcasting systems. Control of program purchasing by noncommercial agents affects the international competitiveness of a country's domestically produced programs and films in two ways. First, the public purchasing agent controls total expenditures on programming, which ultimately limits audience appeal. Public agents could spend more or less than commercial broadcasters would spend on programming. If public agencies spend more, this could be an advantage in international trade to programs produced for noncommercial broadcasters. If they spend less, then programs produced in countries with commercial broadcasting will fare better in international competition. Second, public broadcasters may perform better or worse than commercial broadcasters in matching programming to audience tastes. If audiences prefer the programming choices of noncommercial broadcasters over those of the commercial broadcasters, this would give an edge in trade to programs produced for noncommercial broadcasters. If commercial broadcasters select programs with more audience appeal, then, other things held constant, their programs should predominate in trade.

With regard to program expenditures by commercial and noncommercial broadcasters, the evidence strongly suggests that control of programming budgets by governments or noncommercial agencies, which are dependent on public funds, reduces considerably programming expenditures relative to what they would be if broadcasting were commercially supported. Data presented in the next chapter show that the noncommercial European broadcasting systems are considerably underfunded in comparison to American commercial broadcasters. The dramatic increase in prices paid for programs in Italy as commercial broadcasting developed in that country, and for programs in other European countries following recent moves toward privatization of broadcasting, is further evidence of the negative effects of public control of broadcasting on programming expenditures.

While the proposition seems reasonable, one cannot state uncategorically that commercial broadcasters are more effective than noncommercial broadcasters in selecting programming that is suited to audience wants. However, the close linkage between audience appeal, audience size, and profitability would seem to give the edge to commercial broadcasters. It is doubtful that feedback from viewers to programmers that is channeled through a political process could be as immediate or as clearly expressed. However, the motivation of commercial broadcasters to maximize audience size may be countered by the freedom of noncommercial broadcasters to program to smaller audiences that have more intense preferences for less popular fare.

NOTES

1. For a more comprehensive and detailed discussion of earlier academic work on this topic and the related debates in the international political arena, see the excellent article by Jorge Schement, Ibarra Gonzalez, Patricia Lewis, and Rosita Valencia, "The International Flow of Television Programs," *Communication Research* 11, no. 2 (April 1984): 163–82. The reader is also referred to S.W. Head, *World Broadcasting Systems* (Belmont, Calif.: Wadsworth Publishing Company, 1985) Chapter 12.

2. A more accurate statement of the theory of comparative advantage is that international trade is mutually beneficial when nations export the products that they can produce at lower *relative* costs (compared to the cost of producing other products in the same country) than can their trading partners. The fact that relative costs are what matter in the theory of comparative advantage is generally ignored in the literature that discusses the free flow doctrine and the associated free trade economic arguments.

3. Herbert Schiller, *Mass Communications and American Empire* (Boston: Beacon Press, 1969).

4. For example, see the Report on Behalf of the Committee on Youth, Culture, Education, Information and Sport by Deputy M.-J. Pruvot to the European Parliament, "On the Promotion of Film Making in the Community," Working Document 1-504/83, July 15, 1983, pp. 8, 14–15. Similar concerns over American film distributors are the apparent motivation behind the recent EEC legal action against UIP (the European distributor for Paramount, Universal, and MGM/UA) and recommendations by Canada's federal Task Force on Film, which, if implemented, could severely restrict distribution activities of U.S. majors in Canada.

5. Foreign film and television productions that do well in the United States are almost always produced in English by firms from other English-language countries, most notably the United Kingdom, Australia, and Canada.

6. Schement et al., "The International Flow of Television Programs."

7. The European nations in which the charges of unfair competition by American distributors are most frequently raised maintain nationalized broadcasting systems.

8. In fact, those nations that are the most important purchasers of American films and television programs for broadcast on domestic television generally impose fairly strict limits on foreign content in domestic broadcasts, as is documented in Chapter 6.

9. As we show in the next chapter, it seems fairly clear that government broadcasters pay less than competitive prices for television programming and that this reduced revenue flow works to the disadvantage of domestic producers.

10. How American distributors could profit by discriminating against foreign films is not clear. It is never alleged that the major motion picture distributors discriminate against the films of independent

U.S. producers, but there is no apparent reason why foreign films should be treated differently than those made by U.S. independents.

11. The trade model developed in this chapter and in Appendix B belongs to a class of trade models developed in a rapidly growing economics literature that explores trade issues from an industrial organization perspective. Paul Krugman provides an excellent review of this literature in "Industrial Organization and International Trade," NBER Working Paper No. 1957, Cambridge, Mass., June 1986. Our model of trade in video products is similar to the model of trade and investment in R&D that Krugman presents in "Import Protection as Export Promotion: International Competition in the Presence of Oligopolies and Economies of Scale," in H. Kierzkowski, ed., *Monopolistic Competition and International Trade* (Oxford: Clarendon Press, 1984), in that expenditures on public goods play a critical role in determining trade patterns.

12. Schement et al., "The International Flow of Television Programs," p. 172.

13. Ibid.

14. The simultaneous effects of diversity of audience tastes and the number of competing program suppliers on the diversity of programming offered by the television industry is analyzed in Chapter 3 of Owen, Beebe, and Manning, *Television Economics* (Lexington, Mass.: Lexington Books, 1974).

15. This is the first order condition for profit maximization with symmetry among filmmakers.

16. It is also possible to show that as long as the number of filmmakers exceeds two, increasing F will increase c.

17. The effects on trade in films of variation in the language and cultural differences are treated in the context of a formal economic model in Appendix B.

18. To simplify the discussion, we will assume for the remainder of this section that each country has its own language. The basic analysis would be no different if some languages were common to more than one country.

19. By varying film budgets and numbers of filmmakers for the two countries, and then calculating profits iteratively, it can be shown that, given the basic market parameters specified in this example, there is no stable equilibrium with trade between A and B that permits economically viable filmmakers to exist in B unless films in Country B are subsidized. This type of result is not character-

istic of the recent work on intra-industry trade in differentiated products. Trade in differentiated products models (e.g., E. Helpman, "International Trade in the Presence of Product Differentiation, Economies of Scale, and Monopolistic Competition: a Chamberlinian-Heckscher-Ohlin Approach," *Journal of International Economics* 11, no. 3 (August 1981): 305–40; and P.R. Krugman, "Scale Economies, Product Differentiation, and the Pattern of Trade," *American Economic Review* 70, no. 5 (December 1980): 950–59 generally assume a common distribution of consumer preferences among countries. Firms specialize in production of one or a few variants of the product, and this gives rise to intra-industry trade. In this model there is one characteristic of universal appeal (quality) and one characteristic (the language in which the film is recorded) for which the distribution of tastes is country specific. The fact that the characteristic of universal appeal is a public good, in combination with the large market effect on quality discussed above, makes possible a unidirectional flow of trade.

5

AN EXAMINATION OF LINGUISTIC MARKETS:
Size and Potential

In the last chapter we proposed that populations with common languages constitute natural markets for video products.[1] We then developed a model of trade in video products in which trade flows are determined by the demographic characteristics of linguistic populations and the institutional features of the countries where they reside. The analysis predicted certain relationships between the sizes of linguistic markets and the patterns of trade in video products. Here we want to identify the extent to which the predicted relationships are evident in the data on trade and markets. We also explore the implications of the video products trade model for the design of national policies that affect domestic television and film industries.

In comparing linguistic populations as markets for video products, it is useful to distinguish between linguistic populations' potentials as markets and the degree to which these potentials are realized. The video market potential of a linguistic population is largely a function of demographic characteristics, the most important of which are the number of people speaking the language and their incomes. The number of speakers determines the sizes of the potential television and cinema audiences; personal incomes are a critical determinant of the amounts that potential audience members are likely to spend to view video products, such as cassettes, pay cable, and theatrical films, and the amounts that advertisers will be willing to pay to reach viewers through television.

Whether the video market potentials of linguistic populations are realized depends largely on the resident governments' policies towards video industries and, to some extent, on the

83

dispersal of members of linguistic populations among different countries. Government policies determine the translation of the demand for video entertainment into payments to the producers of films and television programs. Producers' revenues, in turn, determine both the numbers and the audience appeal of film and television productions. We compare major linguistic populations as potential markets for films and television programs in the next section of this chapter. We also look at the government policies that affect the realization of these potentials in the subsequent section.

THE POTENTIAL OF LINGUISTIC POPULATIONS AS VIDEO MARKETS

Table 5–1 lists twelve languages, the numbers of people who speak them as first languages, and the populations and GNPs for countries where they are official languages. These languages have the largest numbers of native speakers residing in countries that rely significantly on market mechanisms to order their economic activity. Similarly, the figures shown for numbers of speakers, populations, and GNPs are for market-oriented countries only. This is because, for a variety of reasons, countries that rely on market mechanisms are the primary international purchasers and suppliers of films and television programs for international trade.[2] In addition, government control of the economy severs the link between demographic variables like population and income and the production and consumption of video products, which is central to Chapter 4's trade model.[3]

A comparison of the income and population rankings in Table 5–1 and the countries identified as important exporters of films and television programs in Chapters 2 and 3 is instructive. It is clear that, in general, countries that rank high in film and television program exports are those with principle languages that rank high in the number of worldwide speakers and, especially, in terms of income. For example, the UNESCO film surveys cited in Chapter 2 listed nine countries as the major exporters of films: the United States, France, Italy, India, the

Table 5–1. A Comparison of Linguistic Populations[a]

Language	Number Who Speak (Millions)	Official Language Population (Millions)	1981 GNP[b] (U.S. $ Millions)	Rank by Number Who Speak	Rank by GNP
English	409	702	4,230,375	1	1
Hindi/Urdu	352	825	209,023	2	10
Spanish	265	271	653,958	3	5
Arabic	163	174	328,547	4	7
Bengali	160	97	12,692	5	12
Portugese	157	163	303,465	6	8
Malay/Indonesian	122	187	237,715	7	9
Japanese	121	119	1,185,861	8	2
French	110	140	812,179	9	4
German	101	76	1,017,528	10	3
Punjabi	69	94	29,575	11	11
Italian	62	63	502,306	12	6

Source: *The World Almanac and Book of Facts* (New York: Newspaper Enterprise Association, Inc., 1984); World Bank, *World Tables*, 3d ed., vol. 1 (Baltimore, Md.: Johns Hopkins University Press, 1983).

a. Figures do not include the corresponding amounts for countries with nonmarket economies.

b. GNP figures are slightly understated for some languages because the World Bank did not report income statistics for some of the smallest developing countries.

Soviet Union, the United Kingdom, West Germany, Japan, and Hong Kong. This list also includes the most important international suppliers of television programming: the United States, France, West Germany, and Japan. With the exceptions of the Soviet Union and Hong Kong, these nations are principal countries associated with the languages listed in Table 5–1. However, the bulk of the Soviet Union's film and television exports goes to other communist nations; and Hong Kong, as a British colony, has close ties to English-speaking countries. Hong Kong also supplies films to the many, relatively wealthy Chinese communities outside of China.

The correlation of Table 5–1 with the lists of important film- and television program-exporting countries supports the hypothesis that both the number of speakers and aggregate income are important determinants of success for television programs and films in the international marketplace. These data also suggest that income is the more important of the two factors. The citizens of the most important television-exporting nations are primarily members of the linguistic populations that rank highest in GNP. Moreover, there is a close, though by no means perfect, correlation between the rankings of film-exporting nations in Table 2–2 and the income rankings of linguistic populations in Table 5–1. In general, the correlation of income and population size for linguistic groups with various nations' performances as exporters of video entertainment are consistent with the pattern predicted by the analysis in Chapter 4. This assumes, of course, that there is a close correlation between a linguistic population's potential and actual value as a video market.

From the perspective of Chapter 4's trade model, the dominance of English-language films and television programs in the world trade in video products is clearly predicted by Table 5–1. English ranks first in both number of speakers and income. When these measures of a potential video market are considered jointly, it is obvious that the gap between the potential English-speaking market and other potential language markets is very large. Japanese ranks second among languages in GNP. Yet Japan, which has over 98 percent of the Japanese-speaking population, has a GNP only slightly greater than one quarter of the GNP of countries claiming English as an official language, and the Japanese-speaking population totals less than one third of the English-speaking population. The number of French speakers is 27 percent of the number of English speakers, and the combined GNP of French-speaking countries is less than 20 percent of the total for English-speaking countries. German totals are slightly less than 25 percent of the English totals on both counts. Only Hindi/Urdu and Spanish, at 86 percent and 64 percent, respectively, have speaking populations that are greater than 50 percent of the English-speaking population. But the corresponding GNPs for these two languages are only 5 percent and 15 percent of the GNPs in English-speaking countries.

Of course, the GNP figures in Table 5–1 allow only inexact comparisons of the spending power of various linguistic populations because minority languages are granted official status in some countries. Two or more official languages frequently reflect the existence of a variety of native tongues within a country. Multiple official languages may also reflect a colonial past. Because of the extent of the former British Empire, GNP figures for countries where English is an official language may overstate the income of the English-speaking population in comparison to the incomes indicated for other languages. However, even if the English-speaking population was assumed to be confined to six unambiguously English countries—the United States, Canada, the United Kingdom, Australia, Ireland, and New Zealand—English speakers would still number 336 million, nearly as many as would Hindi/Urdu. In addition, the GNP for these six English-speaking countries is $3.36 trillion, nearly three times the GNP associated with Japanese, which ranks second on the national income scale. With the exception of Hindi/Urdu and Spanish, both of which have small GNPs, the English-speaking population of these six countries still dwarfs the speaking populations for other languages.

The model presented in Chapter 4 also predicted that increases in the number of speakers and in the income of a linguistic population should have a positive effect on the production budgets of films produced in the language of that population. The average film budgets for five countries, reported in Table 5–2, are generally supportive of the model and suggest that the effect of income, in particular, is especially strong. United States films have the highest budgets by far, followed by Japanese, Italian, and French films, all of which have budgets of about the same value. Egyptian film budgets are only about 10 percent of those for French, Italian, and Japanese films. This ordering of budgets closely follows linguistic population rankings by income. English ranks a distant first, followed by Japanese, French, Italian, and Arabic. Linguistic population rankings by number of speakers are English, Arabic, Japanese, French, and Italian. This ordering follows the relationship that would be

Table 5–2. Production Costs of Feature Films.

Country	Year	Cost
U.S. average	1983	$11,800,000[a]
Japanese estimate	1982	1–2million[b]
Italian estimate	1983	1,250,000[c]
Egyptian estimate	1982	120,000[d]
French estimate	1983	
Solely French Produced		1,160,000[e]
French Coproductions		1,294,500[e]

a. Richard Gertner, ed., *International Motion Picture Almanac 1984*, 55th ed. (New York: Quigley Publishing Company, 1984), p.30A.

b. Estimate of Isao Matsuoka, president of Toho Co., second largest distributor in Japan. Reported in "Toho Topper—Japan No Monopoly," *Variety*, May 4,1983, p. 339.

c. Estimate of Luigi De Laurentis, president of the Italian Producers Association and executive committee member of the Italian Motion Picture Association (ANAKA). Reported in "High Cost of Breakeven Put Italo Prods. through Wringer; Mull U.S. Move," *Variety*, May 9, 1984, p. 304.

d. Samir Farid, "Industry Fraught with Problems but Egyptian Pictures Do Well at Home and in Arab Nations," *Variety*, May 4, 1983, p. 469.

e. "France Big on Big-Budgeters; 17 in '83;'Carmen,' 'Saganne' Tops," *Variety*, May 9, 1984, p. 392.

expected from the comparison of film budgets (with the exception of Arabic).

Of course, the effects of income and population on production budgets cannot really be considered separately. Both operate simultaneously, and the total effect on production budgets is probably a multiplicative combination of the effects of each of them. Still, the difference between the Egyptian and Italian film budgets is greater than what would seem to be explainable by differences in market potential alone. When the fact that television broadcast industries—major purchasers of films in other countries—are not well developed in most Arabic nations is combined with the fact that a number of Arabic governments impose severe restrictions on the types of video entertainment that can be enjoyed by their citizens, it may explain why the apparent potential of Arabic-speaking peoples as a linguistic market has not materialized. The vitality of the commercial television industry in Italy may also be the reason why Italian film budgets are comparable to those of France and Japan. The next section of this chapter discusses the factors that limit the extent to which linguistic populations' potentials as video markets are realized.

FACTORS THAT LIMIT THE DEVELOPMENT OF VIDEO MARKETS

A number of factors affect the degree to which the demands of a linguistic population for video entertainment are translated into payments to the suppliers of films and television programs. In general, factors that inhibit monetary expressions of the demand for video entertainment are influenced, either directly or indirectly, by governments. Legal restrictions on film and program content, which are present in all nations to some extent, depress the demand for certain types of entertainment. The restrictions on films and television in some of the Arabic states mentioned above are among the more extreme examples. Restrictions on viewing times and frequency also limit demand. A number of the barriers to trade in video products, discussed in Chapter 6, restrict demand; these, however, are generally targeted at imports. Piracy and other problems with securing copyright protection, barriers to trade as well, may also limit the development of video markets. The consequences of trade barriers are discussed in some detail in Chapter 7.

Government restrictions on commercial television, especially broadcast television, are probably the primary factors that limit the development of non-English linguistic populations as video markets. They also limit the extent to which these peoples can support indigenous film and television production industries. The international film and television industries were described separately in Chapters 2 and 3, but it should be clear that they are intimately linked. Rentals of films to over-the-air broadcasters, cable, and various forms of pay television are major sources of revenue to film producers. In addition, significant economies appear to be realized by firms that produce both films and television programs. This is illustrated by the relationship between film and television program production in the United States. Many of the resources employed in the U.S. motion picture and television industries are common to both. The majors in the U.S. film industry are generally among the key television producers as well. It is not uncommon for an actor to work in both films and television, and the same applies to technical and managerial personnel. It seems clear that government policies that alter the programming demands of broadcasters have a significant impact on both film and television production.

Government policies affect the programming demands of broadcasters in two ways: types of programs broadcast are frequently affected, and the ability to pay for programming may also be altered, generally downward. Both effects may have important consequences for indigenous film and television producers and can determine whether their productions are competitive in international markets.

Governments' regulations limit the extent to which broadcasters take commercial considerations into account in their programming decisions. Most commercial broadcasters are advertiser supported; that is they generate revenue by selling audiences to advertisers. Accordingly, broadcasters try to maximize the audience appeal of their programming. There is therefore a close correlation between viewer satisfaction with programming and the commercial incentives of broadcasters. While the programmers of government-owned, or public, broadcast systems are concerned with entertainment value, other policy concerns are generally reflected in their program choices. If greater audience appeal is an advantage in international markets for television programs, then programs produced in countries where the commercial aspects of programming are important should have an advantage.

It also appears that government-owned and noncommercial public broadcasters generally have smaller program budgets than do commercial broadcasters. This limits the amounts they can pay for programs and therefore the resources that domestic producers will devote to the production of programs and films that might be shown on television. Strict limits on commercials during broadcasts and restrictions on various types of pay television also reduce programming budgets, necessitating the purchase of less expensive programs for commercial broadcasters. Since lower budget productions also generally have less audience appeal, the weakening or elimination of commercial considerations in the selection of television programming by broadcasters within a country may be expected to make films and television programs produced in that country less competitive internationally.

The extent to which the budgets of public broadcasters are held below the levels that might be generated by less restrained, ad-supported commercial broadcasters is illustrated by the comparison of sources of broadcaster support for the United States and European nations in Table 5–3. Television in all but three of the eighteen European countries listed is entirely a public enterprise. Commercial broadcasters exist in the United Kingdom, Italy, and Luxembourg. However, public broadcasters in most of these nations are supported in part by the sale of commercial time. Daily commercial minutes per broadcaster are shown for each country. Commercial time on the public, and even on the private, systems is significantly less than that for U.S. broadcasters.

The figures in the "100% Revenue Equivalent Minutes" column indicate the degree to which the combination of permitted advertising sales and funding through government grants and receiver fees falls short of what might be generated by stations enjoying the same freedom to sell commercials as those in the United States. The revenue equivalent minutes figure is the number of commercial minutes that the system would have to sell daily to generate revenue that is equivalent to what is now received through the combination of sales of commercial time and funds from receiver fees and government allocations (assuming that the price of commercial time remains the same). The ratios of European systems' revenue equivalent minutes to the actual number of commercial minutes provided by U.S. broadcasters are one index of the degree to which European broadcasters' budgets are reduced relative to what they might be if they had the same freedom as broadcasters in the United States to seek commercial support. These ratios range from a low of .04 for

Table 5–3. A Comparison of Television Advertising and Commercial Television Signals in the United States and Europe.

Country	TV Signals	Maximum Commercial Ad (minutes per day)	Ad Revenue as Percentage of Broadcasting Income (1981)	100% Revenue Equivalent Minutes[a]	Average Number of Commercial Signals Received per TV Receiver
United States	Public broadcasters	0	0	—	5.9[b]
	Commercial stations	268.5[c]	100	268.50	
Austria	ORFI	20[d]	42[d]	47.62[d]	0
	ORFII				
Belgium	RTBF I & II	0	0	—	0
	BRI I & II	0	0	—	
Denmark	Radio Denmark	0	0	—	0
Finland	MTV/YLE I	16	80	20.00	0
	MTV/YLE II	9	80	11.25	0
France[e]	TFI	24	61	39.34	0
	A2	24	53	45.38	
	FR3	10	13	76.92	
West Germany[f]	2DF	20	40	50.00	0
	ARD I	20	30	66.66	
	ARD II	0	0	—	
Greece	ERT 1	30	22	136.36	0
	ERT 2	45	25	180.00	
Iceland	Rikisutvarpid-Sjonvarp	16.4(avg.)	33.7	48.66	0

Country	Channel				
Ireland	RTE I	58	48[d]	86.4[g,d]	0
	RTE II	25			
Italy	RAI I	28	23.8	117.65	
	RAI II	28	23.8	117.65	
	RAI III	—	—	—	
	Commercial stations	162[h]	100	162.00	10–15[i]
Luxembourg	RTL	68	100	68.00	2
	RTL-Plus	68	100	68.00	
Netherlands[j]	Channel I	18	25[d]	72[d]	0
	Channel II	18			
Norway	NRK	0	0	—	0
Portugal	RTP	90	43	209.30	0
	RTP II	45	43	104.65	
Spain	TVE I	57	74	77.03	0
	TVE II	42	74	56.76	
	Regional channels[k]	—	—	—	
Sweden	STV I	0	0	—	0
	STV II	0	0	—	0
Switzerland	SRG (German)	20	35	57.14	0
	SRG (French)	20	35	57.14	
	SRG (Italian)	20	35	57.14	
United Kingdom	BBC I	0	0	—	2
	BBC II	0	0	—	
	ITV	90	100	90	
	Channel 4	50	100	50	

Table 5-3. continued.

Sources: European data reported in *Television Without Frontiers: Green Paper on the Establishment of the Common Market for Broadcasting, Especially by Satellite and Cable*, COM (84) 300 final, June 1984, annex 9, p. 2. U.S. data reported in *Arbitron Ratings/ Television/1983-84 Universe Estimates Summary*, and *Television and Cable Factbook*. no. 52, Stations Volume (Washington, D.C.: Television Digest Inc., 1984). Figures on Italian commercial signals from personal contacts in Italy.

a. The number of advertising minutes that would have to be sold daily to provide the equivalent of 1981 broadcasting income. One hundred percent revenue equivalent minutes are calculated as maximum commercial ad minutes per day divided by ad revenue as a percentage of broadcasting income.

b. Estimate for 1983 based on count of commercial television stations in Arbitron markets. This is a conservative estimate since all local U.S. television markets below the top twenty markets having at least four commercial stations were assumed to have only four commercial stations for this calculation. Many of these markets have more than four commercial stations.

c. This calculation is based on limits specified in the Code of the National Association of Broadcasters (NAB) in 1981. The NAB code permitted 9.5 minutes of commercials per hour during the three prime time hours daily and 16 minutes outside the prime time period. An eighteen-hour broadcast day was assumed for the calculation. The legality of the NAB code's restriction on advertising time has since been challenged successfully in court. Total commercial minutes appear to have increased since that time.

d. This figure applies to both public channels.

e. 1983.

f. 1982.

g. Average for the two channels. $86.46 = [(58 + 25) / 2] / .48$.

h. Commercial stations are allowed 15 percent, or 9 minutes of each hour for commercials.

i. This is a very rough estimate. Italians have available 10–15 channels in the south and 15–20 channels in the north. RAI channels are subtracted from these totals to produce the range reported.

j. 1984.

k. Regional channels with advertising introduced in Catalonia and the Basque country in 1983.

Finland's MTY/YLE II to .78 for RTP in Portugal. For most of these broadcasting systems, the ratio is below .5. (The ratios for European commercial broadcasters are also fairly low due to regulations and conventions that limit commercial time.) Of course, these ratios are but rough indicators of the effect that government controls have had on broadcasters' budgets and therefore their ability to rent or purchase high quality programming in Europe. Advertising prices might fall if commercial time is expanded,[4] but the negative effect of an increase in advertising would be offset, possibly to the point of increasing price, by the positive effect of more attractive programming on audience size.

A comparison of domestic revenue figures for films from the United States and Europe provides a second indicator of negative influence that the restrictions on the development of commercial television have had on the financial support for European film and television producers. From Table 2–16 we can see that nontheatrical buyers account for slightly over 50 percent of domestic revenues for U.S. motion pictures. Nontheatrical buyers in Europe contribute only about 10 percent of the revenue earned by European films.[5]

An examination of governments' television policies shows that English-language producers of video programming are favored by liberal government policies toward commercial television in the major English-language countries, particularly the United States. Relatively unrestricted commercial broadcasters clearly dominate television in the United States, the largest English-language country. This is also true in Australia. The commercial broadcasting system is strong in Canada and is becoming a significant force in the United Kingdom. Commercial cable services have also become important purchasers of films and programs in the United States and Canada. Europe lags behind Canada and the United States by about ten years in the development of cable services, primarily as a result of government policies that restrict cabling and the commercial provision of cable programming. Cabling has not yet begun in most of the rest of the world.

Commercial television is also relatively unencumbered by regulation in most Latin American nations, most notably Brazil and Mexico. Japan and Italy are other important countries that have well-developed commercial broadcast systems, although restrictions on networking impose some costs on commercial broadcasters in both nations. For most other countries, the norm is either government ownership or broadcasting provided and controlled by a nonprofit, government-chartered agency.

An implication of the trade model presented in Chapter 4 is that government policies that limit financial expressions of demand for video products will have the same effect on domestic film and television producers as will a reduction in the size of the home market. Such policies will result in lower budget films and television programs that will be less competitive with films and television programs from other countries. Alternatively, a liberalization of regulations on commercial television should make a country's domestic productions more competitive internationally.

How significant a factor is commercial television in determining the ability of programs and films produced in smaller linguistic markets to compete with the imports from the United States? This question cannot be answered definitively, but recent studies of broadcasting in Latin America, and particularly Brazil and Mexico, suggest that commercial television makes a substantial contribution to the financial health and international competitiveness of domestic producers in these nations.[6] Commercial networks dominate television in Brazil and Mexico, and in both countries the popularity and audiences of domestically produced programs have increased (displacing imported programs in the process) as the financial strength of domestic commercial broadcasters has grown. The result has been a diminished audience for programs from the United States. The 1982 audience hours data reported by Antola and Rogers[7] show U.S. programs with 19 percent of the total audience in Brazil, compared with a 78 percent share for Brazilian programs. In Mexico, U.S. programs held 33 percent of the audience, compared with 66 percent captured by Mexican programs. Both Brazil and Mexico are important exporters of television programs in other Latin American countries, and they sell programming on a more limited scale elsewhere in the world as well.

The popularity of American films and television programs relative to domestic productions is viewed as a serious problem in European nations, which, by objective standards, belong to linguistic populations with considerably greater potential as video markets than speakers of Spanish or Portuguese. The Mexican and Brazilian experiences with commercial broadcasting suggest that the competitive problems of European video producers may be, to a large extent, the result of domestic broadcasting policies. There are a variety of justifications for restrictions on the development of commercial television. However, officials responsible for formulating governments' television policies should be aware of the cost, in terms of weakened domestic producers, of limiting the development of the commercial potential of this medium.

NOTES

1. Again we remind the reader that for purposes of determining "home" markets, cultural differences between peoples may have effects similar to linguistic differences. While we recognize the potential importance of cultural differences, we have chosen to simplify the presentation of this analysis by restricting the discussion to linguistic differences. This holds true for the discussion of differences among linguistic populations that follows. The bias introduced by ignoring cultural differences is probably not great since cultural and linguistic similarities and differences among different groups of people are generally closely correlated.

2. The data on the number of people speaking these languages was not sufficiently disaggregated to permit country by country comparisons. Therefore, the figures for numbers of speakers are worldwide totals.

3. Two languages, Mandarin and Russian, would be added to the list in Table 5–1 if it were expanded to include languages spoken primarily in Socialist countries. Mandarin, with 755 million speakers, would rank first for number of speakers while Russian, with 280 million speakers, would rank fourth. Nearly all Mandarin speakers live in China, which, with a 1981 GNP of $297.4 billion, would have ranked tenth on the list in GNP. Ninety-seven percent of the world's Russian speakers reside in the Soviet Union, which, with a 1981 GNP of $1579.0 billion, would have been number two. Sources for figures in this note include those listed for Table 5–1. The source for the 1981 Soviet Union GNP is the U.S. Department of Commerce, Bureau of the Census, *Statistical Abstract of the United States*, 106th ed., 1986.

4. This assumes that the current limited supply of commercial time is sold at market clearing prices. Apparent excess demand for broadcast commercial time in European nations suggests that this is not the case.

5. Andrew Filson, *The Distribution of Films Produced in the Countries of the Community*, (Brussels: Commission of the European Communities, 1980), p. 3.

6. See, in particular, two articles in *Communication Research* 11, no. 2 (April 1984). L. Antola and E.M. Rogers, "Television Flows in Latin America," pp. 183–202; and J.D. Straubhaar, "Brazilian Television: The Decline of American Influence," pp. 221–40.

7. Antola and Rogers, "Television Flows," p. 189.

6

BARRIERS TO TRADE IN MOTION PICTURES AND TELEVISION PROGRAMS

The U.S. media industries have long faced restrictions on their ability to export their products into foreign markets.[1] Barriers to U.S. media exports may be explicit in the sense that they have been codified and are part of a nation's governing laws. Alternatively, trading problems may result from a nation's failure to establish appropriate legal means of protection for U.S. intellectual properties or to enforce the regulations that do exist. Ongoing efforts by the United States to reform trade practices in the media industries and services generally require a fresh review of available data on all these problems. Fortunately, recent studies by various media industries provide comprehensive inventories of nontariff barriers throughout the world. In addition, timely surveys by the U.S. Trade Representative (USTR) and other federal agencies corroborate the industries' summaries and, in some cases, they provide important details.[2] We have supplemented these sources with trade publications such as *Variety, Billboard,* and *Broadcasting;* discussions with industry officials; and the correspondence files of the USTR that relate to actions initiated under Section 301 of the Trade and Tariff Act of 1984. Our tabular summary of the trade barriers reported in these sources is shown as Table 6–1.

LACK OF INTELLECTUAL PROPERTY PROTECTION

The motion picture and television industries maintain that lack of protection for intellectual property is the foremost barrier now faced in overseas markets. The MPEAA reportedly spends

Table 6–1. Summary of Trade Barriers in Video Products.

Country	Lack of Intellectual Property Protection	Quantitative Restrictions, Screen and Television Quotas	Local Work and Local Contract Requirements	Import Quotas and Licensing Arrangements	Discriminatory Taxes	Earnings Restrictions	Subsidies	Government Monopsony	Other
Argentina	X	X	X			X	X		
Australia	X								
Austria	X						X		
Bahamas	X								
Barbados	X								
Belgium	X					X	X		
Bolivia									
Brazil	X	X	X				X		
Burma								X	
Burundi				X		X			
Camaroon	X	X		X	X	X			
Canada	X	X			X	X	X		X
Colombia								X	
Denmark							X		
Dominican Republic	X								
Egypt	X	X		X		X			X
El Salvador						X	X		
Finland			X			X	X		
France	X	X				X			
Germany	X								
Ghana		X				X			
Greece						X			
Guatemala						X			
Guyana									
Haiti	X								
Hong Kong	X								
India	X			X	X	X	X	X	

Country	1	2	3	4	5	6	7	8	9
Indonesia	X		X		X	X			
Iraq	X	X					X		X
Ireland	X	X				X	X		
Italy	X				X	X	X		
Jamaica	X	X					X		
Japan	X	X							
Kenya	X					X	X		X
Korea	X	X			X	X			
Leeward/Windward Islands									
Malaysia	X	X					X		X
Mexico		X				X		X	
Morocco	X							X	
Netherlands	X					X	X		
New Zealand						X	X		
Nicaragua					X	X			
Nigeria	X		X			X			
Norway						X	X		
Pakistan	X				X	X	X	X	X
Philippines	X				X				X
Portugal				X					X
Saudi Arabia	X	X			X	X	X		
Singapore	X	X	X						
South Africa	X				X		X		
Spain	X	X			X		X		
Sri Lanka	X	X					X		
Sweden						X	X		
Switzerland					X	X	X		
Syria						X			
Taiwan	X				X	X	X		
Tanzania						X			
Thailand	X	X			X				
Trinidad	X	X							X
Turkey	X	X					X		
United Kingdom	X	X		X					X
United Kingdom Territories	X	X		X					
Venezuela	X		X		X	X			

$15 million annually in its worldwide fight against the piracy of entertainment products. This association has also indicated that film and video piracy now costs MPEAA members over $200 million per year in Europe alone, and perhaps $1 billion worldwide.[3] In addition, in summarizing the opinions of entertainment industry executives, a recent CBS survey of trade barriers reported that "executives in the motion picture and television, prerecorded entertainment, publishing, and advertising industries believe that *the most serious trade barrier is copyright infringement*" (emphasis in original).[4]

Copyright enforcement problems of varying degrees are encountered in all markets throughout the world. Moreover, the nature and severity of copyright infringement differs among both individual markets and distribution channels. Copyright infringement problems fall into four broad categories: unauthorized public exhibition, print theft, videocassette piracy, and theft of broadcast signals.

The first of these activities, unauthorized public exhibition, has been reported to occur primarily in more developed countries. Unauthorized presentations of copyright-protected films and cassettes may take place in hotels, cafes, discos, and so-called vid bars around the globe. The MPEAA reports that unauthorized public exhibition of its films occurs in Argentina, Australia, Austria, Brazil, Canada, France, West Germany, India, Japan, South Africa, Spain, and the United Kingdom.

A second, related category of copyright infringement is the actual theft of film prints themselves. Print theft can occur at different stages in the film distribution process. In France, for example, the MPEAA reports that foreign exhibitors sometimes do not return released copies of prints to producers after distribution. In addition, copies of prints intended for distribution may be misappropriated. Finally, prints can be stolen at various stages of distribution, and the negatives can subsequently be used to produce unauthorized prints. MPEAA reports that print theft has become a serious problem in Italy, Spain, and the United Kingdom. The association has indicated, for example, that pirated film prints are shown frequently in Italy by Italian independent television stations.

The third, and perhaps most widespread, form of copyright infringement is videocassette piracy, which has become a global phenomenon. Table 6–2 shows MPEAA's estimates of the percentage market shares achieved by pirated videocassettes in individual markets.[5] As the table indicates, the market shares achieved by pirated videocassettes range from 20 percent in such major markets as Australia, Canada, and France to 100 percent in Brazil, Colombia, and Mexico.[6] From the American distributors' point of view, these markets are not insignificant. MPEAA estimates that in Brazil, for example, over one million pirated cassettes were available as of the end of 1984. Plainly, the piracy of videocassettes is a serious, worldwide problem for the U.S. motion picture industry.

Imports of unauthorized videocassettes into third-party nations also presents a serious problem for U.S. distributors. Table 6–3 shows the origins and destinations of unauthorized cassettes according to the MPEAA. As the table indicates, the United Kingdom and other EEC countries appear to be major sources of unauthorized cassettes flowing to Australia, Austria, Ireland, and South Africa. Indeed, the absence of normal customs

Table 6–2. MPEAA Estimates of Market Shares Achieved by Pirated Videocassettes.

Percent Share	Countries
100[a]	Brazil, Colombia, Mexico, Taiwan
65	Spain
60	Netherlands
45	West Germany
40	Ireland
35	United Kingdom, Belgium
30	Austria, Venezuela
20	Australia, Canada, France
12	South Africa
10	Hong Kong, Italy, Japan

Source: MPEAA, *Report to the United States Trade Representative: Trade Restrictions Facing U.S. Film Producers Abroad* (Washington, D.C.: MPEAA, April 4, 1985).

a. No MPEAA member company has released legitimate cassettes in these markets.

Table 6–3. MPEAA Estimates of Origin and Destination of Unauthorized Videocassettes (parallel imports).

From	To
United Kingdom, Singapore	Australia
West Germany	Australia
United Kingdom, other EEC countries	Belgium
United States	Brazil
Puerto Rico, Venezuela, Panama, United States	Colombia
United Kingdom, United States	Ireland
United Kingdom	South Africa
United Kingdom, West Germany	Spain

Source: MPEAA, *Report to the United States Trade Representative: Trade Restrictions Facing U.S. Film Producers Abroad* (Washington D.C.: MPEAA, April 4, 1985).

restrictions within the EEC may exacerbate this problem as unauthorized (as well as pirated) videocassettes can traverse European borders virtually without hindrance.

The final category of copyright infringement involves theft of broadcast signals. Piracy of this type is most widespread in the Caribbean Basin countries. According to MPEAA, theft of satellite signals by unlicensed homeowner television receive-only (RO) stations is common in the Bahamas, Barbados, the Dominican Republic, the Dutch territories of St. Martin and Aruba, Haiti, Jamaica, the Leeward and Windward islands of Antigua, Grenada, St. Lucia, and Trinidad, and the U.K. territories of Anguilla, Bermuda, St. Kitts, Nevis, and Virgin Gorda. Satellite theft is not restricted to homeowners and other private parties in the Caribbean Basin, however. CBS reports that the Jamaica Broadcasting Company has intercepted such premium satellite programming as HBO and various WTBS offerings in order to retransmit these signals to its viewers without authorization. Without effective signal scrambling, the potential for this kind of abuse almost certainly will increase as satellite transmission of TV programming grows around the world.

Of course, broadcast piracy can affect terrestrial signals as easily as it affects satellite programming. Various cable systems in Canada have engaged in the unauthorized retransmission of U.S. broadcasts. Under Canadian copyright law, U.S. copyright owners were denied both the right to prohibit program retransmission and the right to request compensation for unauthorized program retransmission. The Canadian example highlights the importance of U.S. government involvement in the strengthening of copyright protection for U.S. copyright holders around the globe.

QUANTITATIVE RESTRICTIONS

Screen quotas may be the oldest form of trade barriers faced by the motion picture industry. Screen quotas and other quantitative restrictions are also perhaps the most carefully sanctioned barrier presently recognized in international law.[7] Screen quotas frequently prescribe a specific number of exhibition days for films of local origin or restrict the number of foreign films shown each year. Certain countries, such as Colombia, also require the exhibition of locally produced newsreels and short subjects on any double bill where U.S. films are featured. While screen quotas for motion pictures seem to be losing popularity in many of the developed countries, they remain common in such developing countries as Brazil, Egypt, Indonesia, South Korea, Mexico, Pakistan, the Philippines, Sri Lanka, and Venezuela. In addition, certain forms of quantitative restrictions still exist in Argentina, Greece, Italy, Spain, and the United Kingdom. For example, upon its entrance into the EEC, Spain established new screening rules for Spanish, EEC, and "Third Country" films. The rules require that for every two days that Third Country films are shown, a Spanish or EEC film must be shown for one day.[8]

The severity of screen quotas varies widely from market to market. In Argentina, for example, a theater may be required to show anywhere from four to sixteen Argentine films per year. In Brazil, local features must be shown for at least 140 days per year. By contrast, the government in Greece requires only that first-run theaters in Athens and Thessalonica exhibit Greek films for one week in every three-month period. Thus the impact of these restrictions on the American motion picture industry can be gauged on a case-by-case basis only.

Quantitative restrictions on television programming, including broadcasts of feature films, have also been reported in major markets around the world. In Canada, for example, privately owned broadcast stations must show Canadian programming at least 60 percent of the time during the day and at least 50 percent of the time from 6:00 P.M. to 12:00 P.M. The state-run Canadian Broadcast Company requires a minimum of 60 percent of Canadian programming overall, but it carries closer to 70 percent. The CBS survey reports that in both the United Kingdom and Australia, foreign programming is restricted to no more than 14 percent of total broadcast programming. In France, foreign-made television programs are limited to 12 percent of broadcast airtime, while in West Germany, foreign television can account for no more than 22 percent of airtime.[9] The MPEAA reports that Colombia and Italy also maintain various limits on the quantity of foreign television available to their viewers. In Colombia, for example, a 45 percent limit on foreign programming has been imposed, while in Italy, 25 percent of broadcast time must be allocated to either EEC or Italian television programming. Since, in practice, restrictions on "foreign" programming are tantamount to restrictions on U.S. television programming, the impact that these limits have on U.S. program producers is clearly substantial.

IMPORT RESTRICTIONS

According to the MPEAA report, restrictions on film imports currently affect markets in Burundi, Cameroon, Egypt, Indonesia, South Korea, Switzerland, and the Republic of China. In addition, burdensome licensing arrangements have been reported in India and Spain. In Sri Lanka, all film imports are handled by the state-run national film corporation, while in Syria, the film-importing practices of the government's public cinema organization have lead MPEAA member companies to boycott all film trade with that country. While film import quotas directly harm American distributors, it should be recognized that even *changes* in the allocation of quotas among American film producers can produce indirect, and perhaps less obvious, consequences. A noteworthy example occurred recently when the Republic of China changed its import allocation. This change resulted in what appears to be the first Section 301 action ever filed by the MPEAA with the USTR's office.[10]

Since 1954 the Republic of China's Government Information Office (GIO) has administered film quotas for foreign-produced motion pictures. These quotas were divided into seven major categories prior to 1983. However, the number of allowed imported films in category one—U.S. films by U.S. producers—fell from 171 in 1965–66 to 85 in 1982–83. According to the GIO, each year the designated import quota is furnished directly to the American Chamber of Commerce in Taipei, which, in turn, informs the MPEAA. MPEAA members maintain shared distribution offices in the Republic of China, while independent filmmakers, as a general rule, do not. In 1983 the GIO reduced the category one allocation from 85 to 50. Simultaneously, the GIO established a new quota category that reassigned films from category one to Chinese distributors of U.S. pictures. As a result, the distribution subsidiaries of the MPEAA member companies stood to lose the substantial profits gained through the release of U.S. motion pictures, despite the absence of any *explicit* penalty against foreign-owned film distributors in the Republic of China.

The Republic of China is also a thriving market for pirated videocassettes (see Table 6–2). For this reason, U.S. distributors were already facing entrenched competition from pirated videocassettes, even as the GIO's new quota plan was promulgated. Accordingly, the GIO program exacerbated existing threats to the integrity of the local film distribution release process. While the matter was eventually settled in negotiations, the intensity of the U.S. distributor's reaction does, we believe, illustrate the vulnerability of the international film distribution process to trade barriers.

LOCAL WORK REQUIREMENTS

MPEAA reports that requirements to produce local prints or to dub films into native languages exist in Argentina, Brazil, France, Indonesia, Italy, Mexico, and Portugal. The Argentine requirements are illustrative in this regard. The government mandates that all prints of black and white films to be exhibited in Argentina must be printed locally. In addition, 80 percent of all imported and exhibited colored titles must be made by local authorities, with the exception of one print per title.

In some cases, local work requirements may be both formal and informal. The government of France, for example, explicitly requires that all films released there be dubbed in France or in a French-speaking country of the EEC. However, local print requirements are less explicit. According to the MPEAA, high import charges and informal government pressure have led member companies to manufacture locally all prints used in the French market.

DISCRIMINATORY TAXES

While the MPEAA characterizes film taxes as excessive in a number of countries, the extent to which these taxes are discriminatory is less clear. Nevertheless, the Association reports excessive taxes in India, Pakistan, the Philippines, Singapore, and Thailand.[11] In addition, certain countries maintain film taxing plans that clearly discriminate against foreign motion pictures. In New Zealand, for example, the "film hire tax" is assessed at a higher rate for non-British films than for British films. In addition, branch companies of major distributors that are incorporated outside of New Zealand pay a higher rate of income tax than do companies that are incorporated in New Zealand. The MPEAA also reports a discriminatory admission tax on foreign films in the Republic of China, where U.S. films are subject to a local admission tax of 35 percent, while domestic films are taxed at six percent. Finally, in some countries, such as

Spain, discriminatory film taxes may be imposed on film dubbing activities rather than on film exhibition.[12]

SUBSIDIES

Many governments around the world subsidize their local motion picture industries. Many of these subsidies are funded through admission taxes. Argentina, Brazil, Denmark, France, Italy, Portugal, Sweden, and the United Kingdom finance film production subsidies, at least in part, with admission taxes. "Contributions" from local importers of foreign films are solicited to subsidize local production in South Korea. According to the USTR, these contributions are set at a rate of $172,000 per film, to be earmarked for the "Fund for the Promotion of the Korean Film Industry." In the Republic of China, U.S. filmmakers must contribute $5,000 per film to a similar fund.

Subsidies are funded through other means as well. In Finland, for example, a tax is imposed on the sale of all blank cassettes to fund local production. In France, license fees are imposed on televisions and VCRs for the same purpose. Several countries, including Argentina and Belgium, allow tax rebates to exhibitors of locally produced films. Finally, a number of governments provide various film loans, grants, and prizes to encourage local film production. Countries in this category include Austria, Canada, France, India, Italy, Japan, Mexico, the Netherlands, Norway, South Africa, Spain, Switzerland, and the United Kingdom. While the extent of these payments varies widely, the subsidies can, in some cases, be quite remunerative. In Japan, for example, the ten "most worthwhile" locally produced films each receive 100 million yen (about $400,000) annually. In certain countries, subsidies may be "nested" such that local cities or states impose box office taxes, in addition to federal government taxes, to fund subsidies. In Brazil, the state of Gaunabara and the city of São Paulo both impose box office levies that support production subsidies.

EARNINGS REMITTANCE RESTRICTIONS

U.S. film distributors face various earnings remittance restrictions around the world. Actual blockage of funds has been reported in Argentina, Bolivia, Colombia, El Salvador, Greece, Guatemala, Guinea, Kenya, Nicaragua, Portugal, Sri Lanka, Tanzania, Trinidad, and Venezuela. While blockage of earnings remittances is somewhat capricious in many countries, formal government policies usually establish the level of earnings blockage that the film industry may experience annually. In some countries, such as Sri Lanka, the federal government allocates a fixed amount of foreign exchange each year for film transactions. Any remittances due MPEAA members that are in excess of the authorized remittable amounts must be transferred to a "non-resident block account," which can be used only to offset local expenses. Other countries may establish remittance limits that are based on corporate income performance. In Egypt, for example, remittables are limited to 50 percent of gross income and may not exceed 60 percent of net income. Earnings restrictions of some kind have been reported in the countries of Burundi, Cameroon, Colombia, Finland, Egypt, Guinea, India, Morocco, Nigeria, Norway, the Philippines, Portugal, Taiwan, Turkey, and Venezuela.

While the above lists suggest that the developed countries of Western Europe do not restrict the earnings of U.S. films, it must be emphasized that these countries maintain policies that directly influence earnings, albeit through means other than direct restrictions of remittances. For example, Belgium, Finland, France, Greece, and the Netherlands all attempt to influence film rental terms in some form or other. Within these countries, such bodies as the French Centre National de la Cinématographie set forth, through regulations, the terms under which films may be rented to local exhibitors. While outright blockage of funds may be commonplace only in less developed nations, government establishment of film rental terms in developed countries also reduces the ultimate profitability of U.S. films.

GOVERNMENT MONOPSONY

The MPEAA summary reports surprisingly few instances of the direct exercise of market power through government monopsony of the film-purchasing function. While this result may reflect MPEAA's greater concern with film distribution over television distribution, we believe this question is in need of further research before definitive conclusions can be reached. MPEAA reports that in Burma a government agency that is responsible for film acquisition and development is the ultimate purchaser of all MPEAA member films. In India and Pakistan, imported films can be marketed only through national film-development corporations, while in Mexico, one of the largest theater exhibition circuits in the country is owned by the government. The CBS survey reported that "fifty-three percent of the executives surveyed cited government owned or subsidized distribution and production systems as a trade barrier."[13] The executives indicated that for the motion picture and television industries, government ownership or subsidy was a primary problem in Algeria, Australia, Brazil, Burma, Canada, Egypt, France, India, Iraq, Kenya, Morocco, Pakistan, the People's Republic of China, Sri Lanka, Syria, Thailand, the Soviet Union, and several Eastern bloc countries. Many of these countries also impose explicit quotas on foreign programming. Of course, for the majority of the world's television broadcast systems, which are not privately owned, it is not possible to distinguish between the effects of government or public ownership and those of other barriers, such as formal restrictions on the amount of foreign-originated programming .

OTHER BARRIERS

In addition to the primary categories of barriers, industry sources have described several barriers that, while less widespread than those already discussed, are nevertheless significant to the motion picture companies. In certain countries, for example, dubbing restrictions (as compared with dubbing taxes)

111

burden U.S. motion picture distributors. In Canada, the province of Quebec requires that a French-dubbed version be released within sixty days of any English-language film release. In Portugal, dubbing is flatly prohibited without the permission of the Portuguese Film Institute. Finally, in Egypt, no more than three feature films per year may be dubbed into Arabic.

Other nations impose outright bans on the establishment or maintenance of film distribution subsidiaries. In the countries of Iraq and South Korea, for example, foreign distribution branches or subsidiaries are simply prohibited, while in Nigeria, film distribution companies must be 100 percent "locally" owned. In other countries, restrictions on U.S.-owned film distribution companies seem to be increasing. In Canada, for example, the Canadian Film Industry Task Force recently recommended that the Canadian distribution arms of the U.S. majors be allowed to handle only films for which the parent companies owned worldwide distribution rights. Some countries, such as Saudi Arabia, impose an outright ban on the importation of entertainment films. According to the MPEAA, only educational films and motion picture apparatus are allowed entry there.

OBSERVATIONS

While the foregoing discussion has been concerned mainly with describing the trade barriers that are faced by U.S. film distributors, some obvious conclusions become apparent after a brief review of these activities. First, it is clear that many developed nations in Western Europe and the Far East tolerate extensive videocassette piracy. Paradoxically, many of these same nations—particularly in Western Europe—provide extensive subsidies to their local film industries. In addition, many countries impose local programming content requirements for television that are presumably aimed at the same objective: the maintenance of local television and theatrical production companies. Because pirated films and videocassettes clearly undercut *both* locally and U.S.-produced films, continued toleration of film piracy in these countries must reduce the profitability of locally produced films. This necessitates, in turn, larger subsidies and preferences in order to sustain local production. Thus it appears that the Western European economies, in failing to address the need to enforce intellectual property rights with regard to videocassettes, are pursuing a course that is at least somewhat self-defeating.

A related conclusion that emerges from our analysis concerns the question of so-called parallel imports of unauthorized videocassettes in the EEC. As we noted above, the lack of customs barriers among EEC nations exacerbates the problems of unauthorized and pirated videocassettes moving among these nations. The widespread traffic in parallel imports of videocassettes within EEC countries suggests that multilateral rather than bilateral negotiations may prove more fruitful in settling differences and restructuring rules affecting trade in video products with EEC countries, at least concerning copyright issues.

We have observed that screen quotas and other quantitative restrictions still exist in such developing countries as Argentina, Brazil, Egypt, Greece, Indonesia, and South Korea. Yet these nations have also begun to experience the negative effects of widescale video piracy. Furthermore, since quantitative restrictions on theatrical releases increase prices and reduce the supply of legitimate theatrical products, the quantitative restrictions themselves will, over time, stimulate higher levels of film piracy.[14] Because of this, foreign governments may perceive internal or external reasons to strengthen intellectual property protection for U.S. filmmakers. One possible corrective measure would be the reduction or elimination of quantitative restrictions on showings of legitimate imported theatrical releases, thus reducing the price advantage presently held by vendors of pirated films and videocassettes. In addition, the same strategy might also be appropriate in the case of quantitative restrictions on imported television programs.

Our discussion of the Republic of China's alteration of its import quotas for American films leads to another realization—that trade barriers can be used to harm U.S. investment in distribution subsidiaries overseas, even if the total number of imported U.S. films does not fall. This makes clear that, in many cases, "trade" issues, such as import quotas, simply cannot be separated from "investment" issues, such as government hindrance of overseas subsidiaries. As we observed, manipulation of import quotas can be used to undermine U.S. distribution activities. In addition, it seems clear that the reverse practice may also occur. Manipulation of a foreign government's policies with respect to the distribution subsidiaries of U.S. films can be used to hinder natural trade flows. A recognition of this interchangeability by U.S. policymakers should constitute one element of an effective U.S. strategy for trade liberalization in the film industry.

Finally, many of the less developed economies appear to restrain film earnings remittances directly, either through somewhat arbitrary blockage of earnings remittances or through more formal policies that restrict remittances beyond certain levels of income. Many developed countries use a somewhat parallel practice in setting film rental terms for U.S. releases. This practice harms U.S. filmmakers in much the same way as does outright blockage because it reduces potential profits from overseas markets. While the need to earn foreign exchange among less developed countries may offer some justification for earnings restrictions in those nations, there appears to be no parallel objective accomplished when a developed country, such as France, dictates rental terms on foreign films. Such a practice also seems inconsistent with the commercial considerations that govern trade in other products and services between most developed countries. For these reasons, the elimination of film rental regulations in developed nations may be one area where negotiations could prove fruitful.

NOTES

1. See, for example, U.S. Department of Commerce, *U.S. Service Industries in World Markets: Current Problems and Further Policy Developments*, 1976, Appendix C, pp. C99–C113.
2. Our primary sources included the following: The Motion Picture Export Association of America, *Report to the United States Trade Representative: Trade Restrictions Facing U.S. Film Producers*

Abroad (Washington, D.C.: MPEAA, 1985); U.S. Trade Representative, *Annual Report on National Trade Estimates, 1985* (Washington, D.C.: U.S. Trade Representative, 1985); and CBS Inc., *Trade Barriers to U.S. Motion Picture and Television, Prerecorded Entertainment, Publishing and Advertising Industries* (New York: CBS Inc., 1984). As regards trade problems relating to copyright infringement, the following report was also quite useful: U.S. Copyright Office, *To Secure Intellectual Property Rights in World Commerce*, September 21, 1984.

3. Jay Stuart, "Mifed Antipiracy Forum Reports Countries Taking Effective Steps," *Variety*, October 29, 1986, p. 35.

4. CBS Inc., *Trade Barriers*, p. 1.

5. The country-by-country assessment of copyright infringement problems reported by MPEAA and in the CBS Inc. survey differ slightly from similar assessments made by the U.S. Copyright Office. All sources agree, however, that videocassette piracy has become a worldwide phenomenon.

6. In addition, the U.S. Copyright Office has concluded that in Saudi Arabia, Kuwait, and Bahrain, virtually the entire market for videocassettes is currently served by distributors of pirated works. The Brazilian situation is unique in that MPEAA members are currently boycotting Brazil.

7. See, for example, General Agreement on Tariffs and Trade (GATT), Article IV (Geneva, 1948).

8. Peter Besas, "Spain's New Decree Implementing EEC's Distrib-Exhib Legislation," *Variety*, June 25, 1986, p. 39.

9. Jean Luc Renaud and Barry R. Litman, "Changing Dynamics of the Overseas Market Place for TV Programming," *Telecommunication Policy* 9, no. 3 (September 1985): 249.

10. Section 301 of the Trade and Tariff Act of 1984 allows American companies to raise formal objections and seek remedies against foreign producers of traded goods and services.

11. In India, MPEAA member company earnings are taxed at rates that range as high as 75 percent, the highest tax faced by these companies anywhere in the world.

12. An interesting variation of discriminatory tax practices in the broadcast industry can also be observed in the case of the recent denial by the Canadian government of tax deductibility for advertising payments to American broadcasters. Payments to Canadian broadcasters retained their tax deductible status. This

action brought about a Section 301 filing by several American broadcasters adjoining Canadian markets.

13. CBS Inc., *Trade Barriers*, p. 21.
14. See Chapter 7 for a more complete treatment of the interaction between trade barriers and film piracy.

THE POLITICAL ECONOMY OF NONTARIFF BARRIERS TO TRADE IN VIDEO PRODUCTS

Nontariff barriers are impediments to trade that are imposed and enforced by governments. Copyright infringement barriers result when governments do not act to safeguard the rights of copyright holders to participate in the revenues generated by their products. From a free trader's perspective, nontariff and copyright infringement barriers are the consequences, respectively, of the governments' sins of commission and omission. Governments must incur costs when enforcing nontariff barriers that otherwise would not have to be borne. However, some governments do not provide the copyright protection deemed necessary by American industries because of the costs associated with doing so. In the first section of this chapter we discuss the objectives (both economic and noneconomic) that barriers to trade in films are designed to serve and the reasons why governments that are supportive of enforceable copyrights in principle may not deem high levels of copyright protection worth the expense. The chapter concludes with an analysis of the economic consequences of barriers.

REASONS FOR BARRIERS

The legitimacy of the barriers to trade in films and television programming erected on behalf of cultural objectives is recognized in numerous international agreements and codes (see Chapter 8 for examples). Restrictions on imported films and television programs may serve one or both of two cultural objectives. First, they may be a censorship tool that keeps out films and programs that a government considers inappropriate.

Barriers erected for this purpose are no different in principle from the domestic content censorship that exists in some form in almost all countries. Second, barriers to imported media products may be erected to promote or protect artistic expressions of a country's own culture. A country may hope that reduced competition will improve the profitability and stimulate the production of more films or television programs by domestic producers. Sometimes it is argued that restrictions on foreign films and programs help to preserve the unique aspects of a country's culture as portrayed by domestic producers. Subsidies to native producers, however, may accomplish the same objective without directly restricting the range of consumer choice.

Nationalism and national pride cannot be ignored as reasons for the protection of domestic video producers. The sentiments that give rise to "Buy American" campaigns also contribute to protectionist legislation in the United States. To some extent, domestic producers will be protected and subsidized simply because they are domestic, especially when their films and television programs are viewed as expressions of national values and culture. Because appeals to cultural and national pride receive sympathy, requests for subsidies and protection will always be presented in those terms, even when the motives for the requests are primarily economic.

To the extent that barriers are attempts at economic regulation, the economic analysis of barriers does not differ in principle from that of regulation in general. While there are several theories of economic regulation, the most widely accepted is the theory articulated by Peltzman,[1] which builds on earlier work by Stigler.[2] In Peltzman's model of regulation, the regulator is an economic agent who designs regulations to maximize political support for himself. Recognizing that there are winners and losers in each regulatory decision, the regulator structures regulatory policies to ensure that the political support received from the winners is greater than that lost from the losers. Several researchers have applied the Peltzman framework to trade issues. Hillman,[3] for example, relied on the Peltzman perspective to develop an economic explanation of the political gains and losses associated with the erection of protectionist barriers for declining industries. Marvel and Ray[4] used an analogous theoretical approach to analyze the effects of the Kennedy Round of tariff reductions in the late 1960s. These authors concluded that the substitution of offsetting NTBs for explicit tariffs undermined many of the benefits traditionally claimed for these negotiations.[5]

Empirical studies of trade barriers across countries are also consistent with the predictions of the Peltzman model. One study,[6] for example, found that countries generally erect trade barriers to protect industries in which they have a comparative disadvantage in trade; they do not, however, protect those in which they have a comparative advantage. The Peltzman framework predicts this pattern. Industries in which domestic producers are at a competitive disadvantage stand to gain the most from protectionist measures. Accordingly, political support can be gained from protecting industries that do not fare well in international competition.

The domestic opportunity advantage enjoyed by American filmmakers and television producers is similar, from a trade perspective, to a comparative advantage in other industries. Since this advantage is so overwhelmingly in favor of American films and television programs, it is hardly surprising that many countries have created barriers to their importation. For analogous reasons, U.S. media industries have traditionally had little need to seek protection from foreign competition.

EFFECTS OF TRADE BARRIERS

It is not realistic to expect the elimination of all nontariff barriers to trade in video products. Therefore it is extremely important that those involved in the negotiation of trade agreements recognize the consequences of options taken and options rejected; that is, effective negotiation requires a thorough understanding of the effects of barriers on the international trade in films and television programs.

Film and television producers are affected by barriers to trade with other nations in two ways, the most obvious of which are the direct restrictive effects that are the immediate, and often intended, consequences of the barriers. For example, a producer whose film is denied access to some countries will earn less than he would otherwise. Similarly, such restrictions as taxes on the box office receipts of foreign films may reduce the earnings of those films, a direct and obvious consequence of the restrictions. Less obvious, but just as real, are the second-round, or indirect, effects that occur as producers and consumers respond to barriers. Trade barriers change the incentives to produce and market films, and filmmakers respond by adjusting their budgets and production schedules. The manner in which the motion picture and television industries make these adjustments results in second-round effects that may increase the total cost of trade barriers to a point that is far beyond the losses attributable to the direct effects. Indirect effects must be weighed along with direct effects in the formulation of trade policy regarding films and television programs.

Direct Effects (NTBs)

The foremost direct consequence of many nontariff barriers, and one that is frequently intended, is a reduction in the sales of imported films and television programs. For example, quantitative restrictions on film imports directly limit the number of American films that may be seen by theatergoers in some foreign markets. Content censorship, quotas on foreign programming in television, and screen quotas that limit the dates during which imported films may be viewed have the same effect. Fewer people view imported films and television programs, and foreign producers earn lower profits.

Restrictions that reduce box office receipts may also reduce distribution earnings for filmmakers who distribute their own products in foreign markets. On the other hand, if domestic distributors handle imported motion pictures and television programs, domestic companies will be adversely affected.

While restrictions on the importation and viewing of imported films and programs reduce export revenues, other barriers increase expenses. Various box office taxes levied by governments on foreign films reduce the filmmakers' profits from the export market. Local work requirements, dubbing taxes, and restrictions on print production yield the same results.

The choice by film- and program-exporting companies to establish their own distribution arms in foreign markets or to use domestic distributors may be influenced by the host countries' laws regarding right of establishment. Foreign movie companies face restrictions or outright prohibitions on self-distribution in a number of countries. Close control over the sequence in which films are released, both geographically and temporally among media, is essential to maximizing the earnings on a film.[7] The unpredictability of major hits, which are so critical to the long-term financial success of film studios, makes this control even more important. The extent to which earnings are reduced depends, among other things, on the host country's copyright laws and the degree to which they are enforced. In addition, earnings are influenced by the ability of producers to encourage practices by domestic distributors that are consistent with the maximization of profits across markets.

Imported films, especially American films, make significant if not dominant contributions to the box office in most countries. Regardless of who distributes imported films, foreign exhibitors are hurt by restrictions on the availability of imported movies and by restrictions that interfere with the optimal timing of releases. Restrictions that limit the numbers and viewing of imported films therefore can reduce significantly the earnings of exhibitors.

Foreign filmgoers and television audiences are the obvious losers when restrictions are placed on imported films and programs. For reasons discussed in Chapters 4 and 5, American films and television programs generally have greater audience appeal than do films from smaller countries. Theatergoers have demonstrated by their ticket purchases, as have television audiences by their viewing habits, the strong appeal of imported films and programs. Restrictions on imported products limit both the quantity and the variety of the films and television programming from which an audience can choose.

Domestic producers in restricted markets are the obvious intended beneficiaries of restrictions on imported films and programs. Imported films and programs compete with domestic products for cinema and television audiences. Restrictions on imports therefore boost the audience shares and *may* increase the earnings on domestic films and television programs. However, as we will discuss, because imported films contribute substantially to the financial health of the exhibition industries in many countries, barriers to the importation of films may ultimately prove harmful to domestic filmmakers. Similarly, to the extent that imported programs contribute to the financial health of television broadcasters, domestic producers may also be harmed by restrictions on imported television programs.

Direct Effects (Intellectual Property Problems)

Exporters of films and television programs are adversely affected by two problems associated with the enforcement of rights to exploit intellectual property. The first problem involves copyright laws, which, in some countries, do not provide sufficient property rights for intellectual properties to enable imported films and television programs to generate adequate revenues.[8] The second problem is that lax enforcement of copyright laws, or even tacit approval of copyright violations, encourages film piracy that also restricts the earning potential of films and television programs in some countries. In the worst cases, competition from pirates has made certain channels of distribution, most notably cassettes, unavailable to authorized distributors (see Table 6–2).

Even in countries where the normal distribution channels can be maintained, losses due to piracy are often substantial. Theatrical exhibition and legitimate cassettes compete with illegal copies of films that are shown in theaters and, more importantly, with pirated cassettes that are produced domestically or imported. The MPEAA estimates that film piracy costs its members approximately $1 billion in revenue annually. This estimate does not include sales that would have been made in countries where distribution of a legitimate product was not attempted.

Ideally, distribution starts with theatrical release in first-run theaters; it then proceeds to cassettes, cable, broadcast television, and other outlets. Similarly, there is a preferred sequence for releasing films among countries. Piracy interrupts the preferred timing of release across the media and among countries. Pirated cassettes of a film frequently compete with the theatrical release long before the film normally would be released for cassette distribution. Pirate cassette versions are sometimes available even before theatrical release, reducing earnings at the theatrical stage of release still further. The presence of pirated cassettes, which generally sell below the price of the legitimate product, also cuts into the copyright holder's earnings from cassette sales. The value of the film for release to cable and broadcast television also declines because viewers have already seen the pirated version. The cost to American filmmakers and distributors of the deviations from preferred distribution strategies, such as early releases of cassette versions of films, that are necessary responses to piracy and other copyright problems has not been measured, but it is certainly significant.

Because they too must compete with pirated films and cassettes, foreign film producers are probably also hurt by piracy. However, because American films have universal appeal, they are more likely than domestically produced films to be copied illegally. Because a pirated cassette version reduces a film's appeal at the box office, foreign filmmakers may benefit from reduced competition. Individuals and firms that are engaged in the legitimate distribution of American films are certainly harmed by piracy and the inadequate copyright laws that reduce the demand for films distributed through legitimate channels.

It is not obvious whether the *direct* effects of piracy and inadequate legal protection of copyrights are harmful or beneficial to foreign film consumers. Piracy, on the one hand, enables the foreign consumer to view American films earlier and at a lower cost than would otherwise be possible. On the other hand, pirated copies are likely to be of lower technical quality. In addition, some films will not be made available, and the availability of films through certain channels of distribution may be curtailed or eliminated entirely.

Second-Round Effects

The most important second-round effects of trade barriers, whether NTBs or copyright problems, occur because barriers reduce the potential export earnings of films and television programs. From the analysis in Chapter 4 we know that the number of films or television programs produced and the size of budgets (and thus audience appeal) are directly related to potential earnings. Producers will respond to a reduction in anticipated revenues by producing fewer and lower budget projects. An immediate consequence of a cutback in production would be less employment in the film and/or television industries.

A contraction due to lowered potential earnings would not end with the initial reduction in budgets and output, however. Lower budgets and less varied productions will generate smaller audiences, reducing revenues even more. Budgets would then be reduced again in response to the declining audience, which would produce additional audience declines, which would stimulate further reductions in budgets, and so on. This downward spiral would eventually end in a new equilibrium with lower industry revenue and the production of fewer and lower budget films or programs.

An estimate of the magnitude of the second-round effects of trade barriers on film and television program producers in various countries is beyond the scope of this study. For all but the few countries that are significant exporters of films and television programs, the effect has to be small. U.S. producers, film producers especially, depend on foreign sales for a larger fraction of their revenue than do producers in other countries. Therefore, the U.S. industries that are producing video products are probably most affected by barriers. Because no individual country accounts for a large fraction of the earnings of the U.S. film and television program industries, it is unlikely that the barriers of any one country have a noticeable impact on the number and quality of

U.S. films and television programs. In the aggregate, however, it is likely that the cumulative effect of the barriers of all countries is to curtail significantly output and employment in the U.S. production industries.

Whether or not foreign producers benefit from the barriers that their governments erect to imported films and television programs is not clear. They certainly benefit if the number and quality of competing imports are reduced by the barriers. However, the domestic film distribution/exhibition networks and the television stations that they depend on may be hurt by the loss of the audiences that would have been attracted by imported films and programs. The loss of significant numbers of film exhibitors and television stations conceivably could cause damages to domestic producers greater than the benefits of reduced competition. The event that domestic producers might be hurt by restrictions on imported productions is more likely for films than for television programs. Imported films, especially American films, are responsible for a large share of box office revenues in many countries. One European media official has argued that American films are essential to the health of the film exhibition industry in his country.[9] Whether similar dependencies exist for television programs is less clear as television stations are owned by the government or public agencies in many countries, making their continued existence less dependent on the commercial potential of their programming.

THE RELATIONSHIP BETWEEN NTBS AND VIDEO PIRACY

The issues of video piracy and nontariff barriers to trade in films cannot be treated separately. Trade negotiators must recognize this fact. The relationship between video piracy and NTBs should also be an important consideration for government officials who are responsible for establishing copyright policies.

Video piracy is a supply-side response to consumers' demands for films or television programs. When government restrictions prevent satisfaction of those demands, pirates step in to try to supply what has been proscribed. NTBs imposed to protect domestic producers must therefore be at least somewhat self-defeating, since restrictions on imported films and programs increase the demand for pirated products, which compete with the domestic product. Piracy thus undercuts the protection afforded by NTBs.

Piracy was not always as great a threat to protectionist objectives as it is today. The development of cheaper duplicating equipment (VCRs) and the growth in satellite transmission of programming, which is easily intercepted, have given film pirates a technological edge that they did not always have.[10] Consequently, the achievement of protectionist goals through NTBs now requires much larger expenditures to control piracy.

NOTES

1. Sam Peltzman, "Toward a More General Theory of Regulation," *Journal of Law and Economics* 19, no. 2 (August 1976): 211–40.
2. George J. Stigler, "The Theory of Economic Regulation," *Bell Journal of Economics* 2, no. 1 (Spring 1971): 3–21.
3. Arye L. Hillman, "Declining Industries and Political-Support Protectionist Motives," *American Economic Review* 72, no. 5 (December 1982): 1180–87.
4. Howard P. Marvel, and Edward J. Ray, "The Kennedy Round: Evidence on the Regulation of International Trade in the United States," *American Economic Review* 73, no. 1 (March 1983): 190–97.
5. See also William A. Brock and Stephen P. Magee, "The Economics of Special Interest Politics: The Case of the Tariff," *American Economic Review* 68, no. 2 (May 1978): 246–50; and Jonathon J. Pincus, "Pressure Groups and the Pattern of Tariffs," *Journal of Political Economy* 83, no. 4 (August 1975): 757–78.
6. Edward J. Ray, "The Determinants of Tariff and Non-Tariff Trade Restriction in the United States," *Journal of Political Economy* 89, no. 1 (February 1981): 105–21.
7. Motion picture distributors increase their profits by varying the timing of initial release to purchasers in different distribution channels. Theatrical prices for first-run motion pictures will be

higher if the film has not already been made available in other distribution channels, such as television or videocassettes. Discrimination among purchasers in different distribution channels improves earnings since the distributor can now charge different prices to patrons with varying levels of demand intensity. See David Waterman, "Prerecorded Home Video and the Distribution of Theatrical Feature Films," in Eli M. Noam, ed., *Video Media Competition* (New York: Columbia University Press, 1985), pp. 221–43, for a more complete discussion of the sequencing of releases among different media.

8. For a list of countries with which the United States does not appear to have copyright agreements, see U.S. Copyright Office, *To Secure Property Rights in World Commerce*, September 21, 1984, pp. 74–75.

9. According to François Leotard, French minister of culture and communication, "If the audience for American films in our theaters has grown in recent years, this success has enabled us to maintain in being the network of theaters to which I have just referred, and which is indispensible for the survival of the French Cinema." *Variety*, "French Culture Minister Calling for New Thinking on Pic-TV, Homevid Status," May 21, 1986, p. 43.

10. The development and adoption of effective technologies for scrambling satellite transmissions can be expected to reduce dramatically broadcaster losses due to satellite signal theft.

TRADE AGREEMENTS, INTELLECTUAL PROPERTY AGREEMENTS, AND THE MEDIA INDUSTRIES

The increasing importance of the service industries to the U.S. economy has stimulated both a recognition of the many difficulties faced by these industries overseas and a new interest in using international trade agreements to reduce these difficulties. The growing awareness of the importance of trade in services to the United States and the special nature of the barriers encountered by American services companies is formally recognized in the Trade and Tariff Act of 1984, which authorized the president to afford high priority to the negotiation of bilateral and multilateral agreements in services.[1] Any effort to negotiate trade-in-services agreements must begin, however, with an understanding of existing agreements. The best known and most important of these is GATT, which became effective in January 1948.

GATT

GATT is a multilateral trade agreement involving ninety-one signatory nations. GATT's primary objective is to liberalize world trade through the reduction of tariff duties on traded goods and through the establishment of trading rules and principles that are binding on member nations. GATT is the only contractually binding, multilateral trade agreement in existence, and it affords consultation and dispute settlement procedures for the enforcement of its obligations that have the force of international law.

The most important ("first") principle in GATT is the "most favored nation" (MFN), or nondiscrimination, principle. Under

Article I of GATT, all participating members are bound to grant each other treatment in the application and administration of import and export duties and charges as favorable as those provided to any other country. Thus under GATT no country can provide extraordinary trading advantages to another, with the exception of "special" circumstances, such as regional arrangements or developing countries.

The impact that the MFN principle has had on past efforts to liberalize trade appears somewhat ambiguous. Any nation can delay the process of trade liberalization through the exploitation of the need for a full consensus on trading issues. In addition, GATT's primary reliance on nondiscrimination suggests that "free trade," however defined, is at best only a secondary objective for this trade regime. For these reasons, alternatives to the principle of "unconditional" MFN in GATT will be discussed below.

Article III of GATT summarizes another important concept—"national treatment"—that governs commerce in foreign goods within a country's national borders.[2] National treatment implies that foreign producers will receive the same access to domestic distribution systems as is available to the domestic producers. Under GATT, the parties

> . . . recognize that internal taxes and other internal charges and laws, regulations and requirements affecting the internal sale, offering for sale, purchase, transportation, distribution or use of products, and internal quantitative regulations requiring the mixture, processing or use of products in specified amounts or proportions, should not be applied to imported or domestic products so as to afford protection to domestic production.[3]

In some ways the national treatment language in GATT is less tolerant of protectionism than are the MFN provisions, since MFN requires only that member governments treat foreign goods equally; domestic products might still be favored.[4]

Students of GATT have long recognized that "because the national treatment obligation affects internal governments so directly, it becomes more quickly embroiled in domestic politics than any other GATT obligation and it may be one that is most often breached."[5] Indeed, the importance of the nontariff barriers that violate national treatment obligations has grown dramatically as GATT has succeeded in reducing tariffs.

National treatment under GATT does not encompass "investment" by foreign producers. Indeed, the U.S. government, in its recent study of trade in services, seems to recommend "parallel" attempts to reduce foreign investment barriers in services through multilateral and bilateral regimes other than GATT.[6] Efforts to expand GATT itself would focus on "trade" rather than investment issues. Yet investment is inherent in the provision of many services. For this reason, complete reliance by the major U.S. service industries on efforts to liberalize trade in services through the extension of existing GATT principles may be inadequate. Instead, the service industries and U.S. policymakers might pursue complementary objectives regarding investment through other international forums for negotiation.

GATT sets out in some detail the rights and obligations of contracting parties in the event that differences arise. An aggrieved party may formally charge that GATT benefits have been "nullified or impaired" through the actions of another party. Settlement procedures (of which there are more than thirty) then come into play, obligating the parties to consult in an effort to resolve or minimize disputes. Settlement agreement procedures under GATT generally proceed through five steps:[7]

1. Initial consultations during which the complaining party attempts to settle disputes through bilateral discussion;

2. Establishment and formation of a panel on whose membership and terms of reference the parties in dispute agree;

3. Deliberations during which the panel members request information from the disputing parties and meet to consider arguments and, hopefully, to reach decisions;

4. Consideration of findings and recommendations. If a bilateral settlement cannot be reached, the panel's find-

ings are circulated and then considered in an upcoming meeting of the GATT council; and

5. Follow-up and implementation to ensure that remedies for disputes remain effective.

In its recent review of trade dispute settlements under GATT, the International Trade Commission (ITC) concluded that "the record indicates that existing GATT dispute settlement mechanisms have been adequate for managing all but the most contentious GATT disputes. In many of the more contentious disputes, each stage of the process has been subject to controversy and delays. Establishment and formation of panels has, as a rule, proceeded smoothly, while report adoption and implementation have proven troublesome in recent years."[8] Dispute settlement procedures can still be improved, however. The ITC report identified the various aspects of dispute resolution that need some reform. Nevertheless the commission concluded that the improvement of present trade relations is not dependent on minor procedural changes in the dispute settlement process. Instead, changes in the scope and vision of GATT itself will be needed to achieve meaningful trade reform.

Beyond these "principles," GATT includes a number of related trade concepts that may be relevant to trade-in-services negotiations. One is the idea of "transparency," whereby governments identify and list barriers to trade and notify other countries of changes in laws and regulations affecting trade. The USTR's *U.S. National Study* suggests that, while the process of making transparent rules and regulations that affect services may be more complicated than clarifying NTBs for goods, it is this very difficulty that makes the application of transparency principles even more important for services.[9] Senior Assistant U.S. Trade Representative Geza Feketekuty has called transparency the "first principle" upon which a trade-in-services code should be based.[10]

GATT also provides specific guidance regarding the question of discrimination by state-owned or state-affiliated trading enterprises. Article XVII requires that a GATT member who establishes or maintains a "state enterprise" follow the principles of nondiscrimination in connection with sales or purchases of foreign imports and exports. (This article excludes imports for immediate or ultimate consumption by the government itself.[11])

The last round of trade negotiations (Tokyo Round) under GATT was concluded in 1979. In these discussions, trade in services was granted specific mention for the first time. Of the eight agreements, or "codes," signed by the United States, three had direct or indirect implications for future negotiations in services.[12] The Agreement on Government Procurement, which addresses only the government ministries of the GATT parties, specifically committed these agencies not to discriminate against foreign services when the services are incidental to purchases of foreign goods. This agreement is a large step forward, but GATT still does not cover service contracts per se.[13] However, it does require the parties to consider the possibility of extending this agreement directly to service contracts in the future.

The Agreement on Technical Barriers to Trade addresses questions of the testing and certification standards established by GATT members to ensure safety, health, and environmental protection. This "standards code" provides for MFN treatment and national treatment of imported goods, but it does not cover services directly. The extension of such a standards code to services would seem to have obvious value.[14]

The Customs Valuation Agreement sets forth rules for the calculation of customs values of imported goods. However, the agreement also determines whether charges for some services can be appropriately considered as part of a customs value. Post-importation charges for some services, such as construction, assembly, and maintenance of goods, were deemed excludable from customs valuation.

One important feature common to each "code" negotiated in the Tokyo Round is that a nation may be a party to none, any, or all of these agreements, whether or not it is a signatory to GATT.[15] Accordingly, the Tokyo Round agreements represented, in a real sense, a marked departure from the MFN principle so vital to the original GATT agreement. As we discuss in the next chapter, such variations from the traditional MFN approach may be critical in structuring future trade agreements for the film and television production industries.

OECD CODES

Negotiators need not rely on GATT alone for guidance in the establishment of agreements for the reduction of nontariff barriers. Other models that may be extremely relevant in this context do exist.

The Organization for Economic Cooperation and Development (OECD), for example, has promulgated the Code of Liberalization of Current Invisible Operations (Code of Invisibles) and the Code of Liberalization of Capital Movements. OECD codes are not contractually binding on OECD member countries, but they do offer an opportunity to visualize how liberalization issues in services may ultimately be resolved in more binding agreements.[16] The OECD Code on Invisibles contains a list of "invisible operations," which includes service industries as well as generic business "activities," such as granting of pensions.

Under the Code of Invisibles, OECD members agree to practice general measures of trade liberalization. For example, they agree to simplify the formalities that are connected with the authorization or verification of each "invisible" operation. While the code appears to suffer from the lack of formal dispute-resolution procedures, it does emphasize good-faith application of its principles among members. Unfortunately, the absence of dispute-resolution procedures in what is already a nonbinding agreement reduces the code to little more than a symbolic commitment to liberalization of trade in services. However, as a model for more formal agreements, the OECD code clearly has value. It does consider, for example, the economic impact of a member's "derogation" in deciding whether a particular nation's policy *not* to liberalize treatment of an invisible operation was justified.[17] The code's reliance on an economic impact standard may provide a useful and practical suggestion that should be considered in future trade-in-services regimes.

The OECD Code of Liberalization of Capital Movements does not address services per se. However, it does seek to liberalize restrictions on capital movements among OECD members. According to the *U.S. National Study*, "The Code applies to direct investment and is about to be extended to include those aspects of the right of establishment most closely related to direct investment." This extension is intended to increase transparency and to liberalize the investment measures and restrictions that affect the service industries.[18] It is noteworthy that the OECD efforts aimed at the liberalization of services trade (invisibles) and direct investment (capital movements) have proceeded on separate, but seemingly parallel, tracks. This approach can be contrasted with the apparent decision of the USTR to relegate multinational reform in direct investment restrictions to a secondary status behind reform in services trade.

In addition to the Code of Liberalization of Capital Movements and the Code of Invisibles, OECD publishes occasional reports that clarify the practices of member countries in achieving progress in liberalizing trade. For example, it has released a declaration that relates to international investment and multinational enterprises. Within the declaration, OECD discusses the national treatment of foreign investments. In seeking to clarify the meaning of national treatment in this context, OECD also released an "instrument" entitled National Treatment for Foreign Control Enterprises.[19] This enlightening document offers a definition of national treatment that can be applied in specific circumstances. OECD concludes that treatment that is no less favorable than that accorded *in like situations* to domestic enterprises embodies the spirit of national treatment. However, it also concludes that the expression "in like situations" reflected member concerns that the comparison of treatment given foreign and domestic firms be made solely within the same sector.[20] OECD also stated that the national treatment instrument did not apply to the initial establishment of foreign-controlled companies, although the instrument clearly was interpreted to apply to further investments of foreign-controlled corporations that were already established in the member economy.[21]

FILM INDUSTRY EXCEPTIONS IN GATT
AND OECD

The motion picture industry is the only "service" sector included within the framework of both GATT and the OECD's Code of Invisibles.[22] This unique position appears to stem, at least in part, from a longstanding policy among many nations to maintain a domestic film industry capable of portraying each nation's unique culture and lifestyle. This capability is seen by some nations as the very substance of national identity.[23]

Article IV of GATT specifically permits the establishment or maintenance of film screen quotas to guarantee that a minimum percentage of total screen time will be applied to the exhibition of films of national origin. This exception to the general principle of nondiscrimination is also recognized explicitly in Article III (10)—the national treatment provision, which is so important to the usefulness of GATT. While the GATT exception for films is clearly related to national cultural policies, it has also been suggested that the ability to tap film revenues as a source of government income may have played a critical role in the origin of this article.[24]

Notwithstanding GATT's implied commitment to full national treatment for all foreign motion pictures, with the exception of films that are protected by screen quotas, it is clear that numerous violations of GATT principles occur in all film distribution channels. In 1961 the United States sought to introduce new language into GATT that addressed restrictions by many countries on trade in television programming.[25] The United States representative argued that barriers to free commerce in television violated the spirit, if not the letter, of GATT rules, and he sought to add a clarifying GATT article to address this problem. No action has been taken on this proposal to date.

The OECD Code of Invisibles also contains numerous exceptions to the general principles of trade liberalization for motion pictures. Annex IV to Annex A of the code specifically allows these exceptions, holding that: "For cultural reasons, systems of aid to the production of printed films for cinema exhibition may be maintained *provided that they do not signif-*

icantly distort international competition in export markets [emphasis added]."[26]

The Code of Invisibles states that screen quotas may be maintained as an appropriate aid to domestic production, while discriminatory "duties, deposits, or taxes" are prohibited. This code also provides that co-produced films be afforded nondiscriminatory treatment.

In language that is somewhat similar to that found in the Code of Invisibles, the OECD national treatment instrument lists many exceptions pertaining to the motion picture industry. For example, official aids and subsidies are available for film production industries in Australia, Italy, Switzerland, and the United Kingdom. Other exceptions relating to the film industry include the Australian government's provision of tax deductions for capital expenditures on qualifying Australian films and the Swiss government's prohibition on the distribution of motion pictures by companies that are not Swiss owned. In addition, many nations enforce barriers on ownership of cable and broadcast television facilities as well as on broadcast rights.[27]

EUROPEAN ECONOMIC COMMUNITY

Multinational treaty provisions that address trade in media services have not been limited to the global trade agreements discussed above. Indeed, one of the most ambitious efforts to liberalize international trade in video products has been undertaken within the regional confines of the EEC. This effort achieved widespread publicity with the 1984 release of the Commission of the European Communities' Green Paper, *Television Without Frontiers.*[28]

The Green Paper provides a set of policy guidelines for the eventual elimination of barriers to transborder television broadcasting in the EEC. As such, the report focuses on barriers within the community rather than on trade with noncommunity nations. Indeed, the Green Paper's stated goals seem quite protectionist from the viewpoint of noncommunity, particularly American, television products.

137

... most of the films shown (on European television) come from one single non-member country—the USA. As a result, there is already a certain uniformity in the range of films screened on television in the Community. Programs such as "Dallas" are carried by almost every television channel in the Member States. The creation of a common market for television production is thus one essential step if the dominance of the American media corporations is to be counter balanced.[29]

Other EEC documents and working papers confirm this protectionist sentiment, citing large market shares by U.S. television producers as justification for the establishment of new community-wide aid programs for television and cinema in Europe.[30]

One of the more controversial proposals set forth in the Green Paper was the apparent recommendation to allow immediate, cross-border, cable retransmission of copyright-protected programming that was already being broadcast anywhere in the EEC. This implicit "compulsory license" was roundly criticized by copyright holders, and in a 1986 draft directive from the Council of Ministers of the EEC, the commission revised its original intentions somewhat.[31] In its directive, the commission offered a two-year period of negotiations between broadcasters and program producers prior to the imposition of a statutory license.[32] While program producers seemed to welcome the commission's directive, further attempts to change this proposal continue at this writing.

The European cross-border broadcast proposals are, in our view, useful models in spite of these limitations. The Green Paper provides a concrete example of media trade liberalization in practice. It represents paths that might be taken or avoided in global negotiations, and for this reason alone, its importance is unquestionable.

The Green Paper derives its authority from Articles 59 (1) and 62 of the Treaty of Rome. Article 59 (1) requires that restrictions on the freedom to provide services within the community be abolished, while Article 62 prohibits the introduction of new restrictions.[33] The specific recognition of trade in services among nations is, of course, a progressive and desirable feature of the EEC agreement. However, in practice, the application of these provisions to transborder television signals has proven somewhat controversial. After several cases before the Court of Justice, most notably the 1974 *Sacchi* case[34], the relevance of the EEC services trade articles to television broadcasting was established.

The *Sacchi* case involved a challenge to Radio Audizone Italiana (RAI), the Italian state monopoly broadcaster. Giuseppe Sacchi sought to contest the imposition of certain licensing fees on the grounds that RAI's monopoly on broadcast transmission was in conflict with Article 37 of the Treaty of Rome, which restricts the trading in goods of state-owned monopolies. The court decided to treat television broadcasting as a service rather than a good. Following this logic, it denied the applicability of Article 37 to broadcast programming. However, in this case, the court also went on to state that "trade in material, sound recordings, films, apparatus and other products used for the diffusion of television signals" remained subject to the rules relating to freedom of goods rather than services.[35] Thus the court's decision sanctioned different legal standards for various media in Europe. Whatever the ultimate rationale behind this decision, it seems clear that the acceptance of separate legal treatment for films and television media may well distort economic incentives for film and television distributors in the future. Such inefficiencies, of course, reduce consumer welfare. The costs of inefficiences resulting from legal distinctions among media that have no economic basis will certainly grow as European media industries prosper in the new, more liberal environment.

The EEC's broadcast reform efforts are instructive in yet another way. In a 1980 case before the Court of Justice, the *Debauve* case,[36] the court provided a clear example of how potentially innovative trade provisions can be held hostage to the interests of the least reform-minded nations. In this case, the court considered the legality, under EEC regulations, of national rules on advertising that is retransmitted across European borders. The court ruled that, "with regard to the trans frontier broadcasting of advertisements, all discrimination against foreign broadcasts was prohibited."[37] However, nondiscriminatory restrictions—and even complete bans—on the national retransmission of foreign advertising broadcasts that were applied equally to national and foreign services would be permitted under EEC law if two conditions were fulfilled. First, the restrictions must be in the national general interest. Second, restrictions may apply if national laws have not been approximated.[38] In the EEC, "approximation" is the process by which the rules and regulations imposed by individual nations on services are harmonized so that a rough equivalence exists among them. In this way, perceived "legitimate" interests of the general public in each nation can be protected while community-wide broadcast advertising rules are liberalized. Exact conformance of national laws would not be required. In the *Debauve* case, the court held, essentially, that the free dissemination of advertising, which is guaranteed by the EEC treaty, cannot be imposed if national laws have not been approximated.[39] As the European Parliament's Committee on Youth, Culture, Education, Information and Sport soberly observed:

> Because of such reservations [on advertising] there are still, in the final analysis, national inconsistencies, though in theory, these inconsistencies can be attenuated through approximation, experience indicates that, as regards the heart of public-order legislation at least, they virtually defy elimination through harmonization.[40]

The EEC experience with approximation of national laws is relevant to future trade agreements in services. For the EEC, the harmonization of national laws to achieve rough equalization of broadcast transmission regulations would seem to represent a step forward. However, the EEC experience also highlights the vulnerability of trade regimes where a few nations' decisions can delay beneficial reform for the group as a whole. To the extent that this lesson can be applied to such other trade forums as GATT, we suspect that an analogous vulnerability will be recognized. In GATT, the unconditional MFN principle, like the principle of approximation, can, we believe, delay the implementation of trade reform in services. For this reason, the EEC experience might well be taken as evidence in support of a "conditional" type of MFN.[41]

OTHER MODELS

Beyond GATT, OECD, and the EEC provisions, there are numerous bilateral agreements in many services that might be instructive for constructing a trade-in-services regime. While many of these agreements are not particularly important for the motion picture and television program industries,[42] it is illuminating to consider the U.S. view of the relative advantages and disadvantages of bilateral and multilateral trade agreements, as expressed in the *U.S. National Study*. In this study, the USTR concluded that, while bilateral arrangements pertaining to individual sectors are "potentially, the easiest of all undertakings to establish among countries," they have several distinct disadvantages.[43] These disadvantages include the undermining of hope for international "harmony" among nations and the reduction of benefits of trade competition through the possible allocation of market share among trading partners. The study was more optimistic with regard to bilateral trade agreements for all trade sectors, however. While recognizing that no such agreement currently exists, the study concluded that "under a bilateral accord, the balance of concessions made by each country could be more precisely measured in such a way that more liberalized trade in services results and, the balance of concessions could be spread over more than one sector, which generally tends to enhance competitive opportunities for both sides."[44] The study also recognized that bilateral, multisector agreements would involve the wholesale abandonment of the MFN principle in favor of "a preferential system based on reciprocal opportunities."[45]

The *U.S. National Study* falls short of recommending a preferred sectoral approach by service industry officials who are

141

seeking to liberalize trade. Both bilateral and multilateral agreements are seen to offer advantages and disadvantages for the U.S. service industries. It seems clear, however, that a viable strategy for the film and television program industries almost certainly will involve reliance on both types of trade arrangements.

THE BERNE AND UCC AGREEMENTS ON INTELLECTUAL PROPERTY

In attempting to reform trade practices in motion pictures and television, U.S. policymakers must consider more than the historical context surrounding agreements such as GATT and the OECD Code of Invisibles. Given the recent severity of video piracy, it is clear that meaningful reform cannot proceed without an understanding of U.S. copyright law specifically and issues of intellectual property generally.

Copyright law is dominated by two multinational agreements—the Berne Convention and the Universal Copyright Convention (UCC). Berne, the older convention, had seventy-six signatories as of March 1985, while the UCC had seventy-eight. Several bodies exist within these conventions to further the modernization of copyrights internationally. In the Berne Convention, the World Intellectual Property Organization (WIPO) fulfills such a role; UNESCO serves this function in the UCC. Both WIPO and UNESCO are specialized agencies of the United Nations.[46]

The United States is a UCC signatory, but it is not a signatory to the Berne Convention.[47] Current U.S. copyright law still requires that prospective copyright holders satisfy a number of formalities to obtain copyright protection.[48] Since formalities of this nature are flatly inconsistent with the principles of the Berne Convention, the United States is now precluded from Berne Membership.

The philosophical cornerstone underlying both the UCC and the Berne Convention is that national treatment should prevail in all member countries. Under the UCC, for example, works of the nationals of all member countries should be afforded "the same protection as that other State accords to works of its nationals first published in its own territory."[49] While the UCC and the Berne Convention address copyright-related forms of protectionism, they do not consider such noncopyright versions as content quotas, business restrictions, retention or repatriation of foreign earnings, and tax manipulation.

In addition to addressing national treatment, the UCC and the Berne Convention focus on providing adequate and effective protection to works of intellectual property. In the UCC, however, adequate and effective protection is defined generally and relies on simple conceptual language. Thus the extent of protection awarded to a foreign copyright holder is a function of each nation's domestic protection of its own authors. The amount of protection therefore varies widely among states.

During the 1950s and 1960s, U.S. international copyright policy sought to recognize the demands of emerging Third World countries to secure exceptions to the exclusive rights guaranteed to authors. Largely as a result of demands to secure protected works that would aid education and general development, the UCC adopted compulsory licenses. Under these licenses, rights to translate works of intellectual property, or to reprint such works for development, may be presumed after good-faith efforts to secure a voluntary license from the copyright holder have failed. Under compulsory licensing, the copyright holder retains the power to terminate the applicant nation's compulsory license by publishing a comparable edition of the work in the protected territory. In addition, works under compulsory license cannot be exported to third markets.

While the initiation of compulsory licensing programs under the UCC and the Berne Convention may have helped to rebut charges that the international copyright system is unresponsive to developing nations' needs, some copyright owners are concerned that compulsory licenses exist at all. For purposes of this book, however, the most salient feature of compulsory licenses is that they are now embedded in both UCC and Berne Convention procedures. Thus to the extent that future GATT negotiations on video products trade are to consider intellectual property issues, it seems quite possible that claims for special treatment

143

by developing countries might be rationalized on the grounds of the compulsory license precedent established under the UCC and the Berne Convention.

EEC COPYRIGHT PROVISIONS

Despite the seemingly vast differences between GATT and the Berne Convention and UCC copyright agreements, it should be noted that a recognition of the importance of copyright issues in multinational trade agreements is not wholly unknown. Under the Treaty of Rome, ". . . intellectual property rights are as much subject to the EEC treaty as industrial property rights (patents, trademarks, designs and models.)"[50] The EEC agreement is clearly innovative in this regard. As with EEC trade rights, however, the Court of Justice has imposed a legal distinction between copyrights for video services (broadcasting) and copyrights for video goods (cassettes). This distinction can produce anomalous results for cinema and television productions that are released through more than one medium. In the 1980 *Coditel* case,[51] the court held that an assignee of performing rights was not precluded by the EEC treaty from prohibiting unauthorized cable diffusion of a foreign transmission.[52] As with the *Debauve* case, harmonization of national copyright laws was seen as a prerequisite before the full implementation of the relevant EEC provisions could begin. In describing the logical implications of the *Coditel* decision, the Green Paper offered the following hypothetical situation:

> If for example, a copyright owner assigns to firm A the rights, limited to one member state of the community, to broadcast a work and also to record the broadcast on a cassette and market the cassettes in that state, and then assigns to firm B the corresponding rights in another member state, firm A may take action to prevent the broadcast made by firm B from being retransmitted in the area for which firm A has the broadcasting rights, but cannot take any action to prevent the

marketing in A's territory of the broadcast recorded on cassettes by B.[53]

Such discrepancies in the treatment of video works that are disseminated through different media plainly give rise to the possibility of distortions in release patterns for video productions within the EEC.[54] To avoid similar distortions in the global video trade, negotiators should attempt to incorporate a correct understanding of transmedia release patterns in any multinational agreement on intellectual property.

OTHER COPYRIGHT AGREEMENTS

Several, more focused copyright agreements also seem relevant for trade in motion pictures and television programs. Two agreements, the Geneva Phonograms Convention of 1972[55] and the Brussels Satellite Convention of 1974, are especially important. The Phonograms Convention obliges members to protect producers of phonograms who are nationals of other contracting states "against the making of duplicates without the consent of the producer and against the importation of such duplicates, provided that any such making or importation is for the purpose of distribution to the public, and against the distribution of such duplicates to the public."[56] The Phonograms Convention differs from copyright agreements in several important respects. First, the convention applies specifically to *foreign* sound-recording producers. Unlike the UCC and the Berne Convention, however, a country's obligation to protect such property is not based on national treatment.[57] It is thus theoretically possible for a contracting state to protect the sound recordings of foreign producers without protecting domestic producers.

In addition, the Phonograms Convention does not regulate all intellectual property relationships. Rather it seeks only to protect authors against unlawful reproduction for public distribution. The importation of pirated copies of phonograms as personal property is not restricted, and the convention does not

145

restrict the reproduction of sound recordings in the homes of nationals of contracting states. Nevertheless the Phonograms Convention represents, in many ways, an innovative and important milestone in the fight against sound-recording piracy.

One last feature of the Phonograms Convention that is relevant to trade in services concerns the prosecution of recording pirates under Article II:

> the means by which this convention is implemented shall be a matter for the domestic law of each contracting state and shall include one or more of the following: protection by means of the grant of a copyright or other specific right; *protection by means of the law related to unfair competition*; and protection by means of penal sanctions [emphasis added].[58]

The application of domestic laws and sanctions against unfair competition is a useful model for the structuring of future trade-in-services agreements that address the issues of film and video piracy.[59] Acquisition of copyrighted works through piracy might be treated as an "unfair" competitive advantage.

The Brussels Satellite Convention's pact on the distribution of program-carrying signals transmitted by satellite also has relevance to the video products trade. The Satellite Convention seems to have emerged because neither the UCC nor the Berne Convention protected broadcasters or their broadcasts against *international* piracy, although purely domestic broadcasts were already regulated. Accordingly, as satellite technology became more widespread, industry officials realized that satellite signal transmissions would become increasingly vulnerable. The approach taken in the Satellite Convention is comparable to that taken in the Phonograms Convention. A contracting state is obligated "to take adequate measures to protect the distribution on or from its territory of any program-carrying signal by any distributor from whom the signal emitted to or passing through the satellite is not intended."[60] The convention aims to protect program-carrying satellite signals from unauthorized interception and distribution. However, it does not apply to unauthorized distribution of signals subsequent to the authorized terrestrial distribution of a satellite-derived signal.[61] In addition, the Satellite Convention excludes signals intended for direct reception by the general public; these signals are generally protected by copyright or "neighboring rights" regimes in most countries. Finally, the Satellite Convention includes a provision that permits unauthorized distribution of program-carrying signals in a developing country, "provided that distribution is solely for the purpose of teaching including teaching in the framework of adult education, or scientific research."[62]

As a result of certain of these provisions, United States proprietary interests argued that protection under the Satellite Convention would be inadequate and would, in addition, conflict with efforts to reform U.S. domestic copyright law. For this reason, the United States did not ratify the Satellite Convention until October 12, 1984.[63]

NOTES

1. Individual service sectors to be emphasized in these agreements include telecommunications and data processing, engineering, maritime services, banking, insurance, professional services, advertising, tourism, franchising, lodging, aviation, and motion pictures.
2. National treatment applies to goods that have already been subjected to whatever "legitimate" tariffs or quotas apply at the border.
3. General Agreement on Trade and Tariffs (GATT), Part II, Article III, para. 1.
4. John H. Jackson, *World Trade and the Law of GATT* (Bobbs-Merrill Company, 1969), p. 273.
5. Ibid., p. 274.
6. Office of the U.S. Trade Representative (USTR), "U.S. National Study of Trade in Services," December 1983, p. 255.
7. U.S. International Trade Commission, *Review of the Effectiveness of Trade Dispute Settlements Under the GATT and the Tokyo Round Agreements*, Report to the Committee on Finance,

U.S. Senate Investigation No. 332-212, U.S. ITC Publication 1793, December 1985, pp. vi and vii.

8. International Trade Commission, *Effectiveness of Settlements*, p. x.

9. USTR, "U.S. National Study," p. 6.

10. Address by Geza Feketekuty before the University of Michigan Third Annual Workshop on U.S. Canadian Relations, Ann Arbor, Michigan, October 19, 1984, p. 9 (mimeo).

11. GATT, Article XVII, para. 2.

12. The agreements are: (1) The Agreement on Technical Barriers to Trade, (2) The Agreement on the Interpretation and Application of Articles VI, XVI and XXIII of GATT, (3) The Arrangement Regarding Bovine Meat, (4) The Agreement on Implementation of Article VII of GATT, (5) The Agreement on Import License Procedures, (6) The Agreement on Trade in Civil Aircraft, (7) The Agreement on Implementation of Article II, and (8) The Agreement on Government Procurement.

13. USTR, "U.S. National Study", p. 7.

14. Ibid.

15. International Trade Commission, *Effectiveness of Settlements*, pp. 29-30.

16. The OECD codes are further weakened by numerous "reservations" and "derogations" on certain obligations that qualify a nation's intent to adhere to the strict language of each code indefinitely.

17. Such a qualification concerning economic harm is included also in Annex IV to Annex A of the Code of Invisibles dealing with film barriers.

18. USTR, "U.S. National Study," p. 88.

19. Organization for Economic Cooperation and Development (OECD), *National Treatment for Foreign Controlled Enterprises, International Investment and Multinational Enterprises* (Paris: OECD, 1985).

20. Ibid., p. 17.

21. Initial foreign direct investments are covered under the Code of Liberalization of Capital Movements.

22. USTR, "U.S. National Study," p. 255.

23. See, for example, European Parliament, Committee on Youth, Culture, Education, Information and Sport, *For a Regulation on a Community Aid Scheme for ·Non-Documentary Cinema and Television Co-Production*, Document A2-93/85, 1985.

24. Jackson, *World Trade and the Law of GATT*, p. 294, n.

25. USTR, "U.S. National Study," p. 255.

26. OECD, *Code of Liberalization of Current Invisible Operations*, Annex IV to Annex A, para. 1.

27. The United States limits foreign ownership interests in U.S. broadcasting stations to 20 percent.

28. Commission of the European Communities, *Television Without Frontiers: Green Paper on the Establishment of the Common Market for Broadcasting, Especially by Satellite and Cable*, COM (84) 300, Final, June, 1984.

29. Ibid., p. 33.

30. See Committee on Youth, *Community Aid Scheme*.

31. Commission of the European Communities, *Proposal for a Council Directive on the Coordination of Certain Provisions Laid Down by Law, Regulation or Administrative Action in Member States Concerning the Pursuit of Broadcasting Activities*, COM (86) 146 Final/2, April 30, 1986.

32. Ibid., Article 18, p. 33.

33. Committee on Economic and Monetary Affairs and Industrial Policy. *Report on the Economic Aspects of the Common Market for Broadcasting*, A2-102/85, September 30, 1985, p. 25.

34. *Giuseppe Sacchi v. Italian Republic*, E. Comm. Ct., J., No. 155/73 (preliminary ruling), April 30, 1974.

35. Commission of the European Communities, *Green Paper*, pp. 105–06.

36. *Cotidel v. Debauve*, E. Comm. Ct., J., No. 52/79, 1980.

37. European Parliament, Committee on Youth, Culture, Education, Information and Sport, *Green Paper Report*, A2-75/85, July 5, 1985, p. 18.

38. Ibid.

39. Ibid.

40. Ibid.

41. However, we are also sensitive to the potential difficulties involved in code-conditional *broadcast* agreements where bordering nations do not choose to participate.

42. We exclude from this characterization the recent U.S.-Israeli multisector agreement on service trade principles, which may have been the first formal recognition between major nations that services trade barriers are mutually disadvantageous and in need of liberalization.

43. USTR, "U.S. National Study," p. 101.

44. Ibid., p. 103.
45. Ibid.
46. The United States withdrew from UNESCO in late 1984 as a result of perceived increasing politicization of that body in recent years.
47. The United States achieves protection under the Berne Convention through the device of simultaneous release in the United States and in Canada, a Berne signatory.
48. Notice and deposit registration with the U.S. Congress are perhaps the most important formalities.
49. U.S. Congress, Office of Technology Assessment, *Intellectual Property Rights in an Age of Electronics and Information*, OTA-CIT-302 (Washington, D.C.: April 1986), p. 236.
50. Commission of European Communities, *Green Paper*, p. 6.
51. *Coditel v. Cine Vog*, E. Comm. Ct., J., No. 62/79, 1980.
52. Commission of European Communities, *Green Paper*, p. 304.
53. Ibid., pp. 304–305.
54. In this connection, however, the language may be somewhat misleading since national copyrights within the EEC still receive some protection under Article 36 of the Treaty of Rome. Article 36, which addresses the free movement of goods in the European Community, allows an exception to the free movement ideal where the essential function of a particular property right is threatened by the abolition of internal trade frontiers. Thus, the free flow of videocassettes into Firm A's territory might still be protected under national copyright laws.
55. The agreement is formally entitled *The Convention for the Protection of Producers of Phonograms Against Unauthorized Duplication of Their Phonograms*.
56. Article II, *Convention for the Protection of Producers of Phonograms Against Unauthorized Duplication of Their Phonograms*, as quoted in U.S. Copyright Office, *To Secure Intellectual Property Rights in World Commerce*, September 21, 1984, p. 57.
57. U.S. Copyright Office, *Intellectual Property Rights in World Commerce*, p. 58.
58. *Phonogram Convention*, Article II.
59. For a comprehensive list of local remedies available to producers for infringement of rights in cinematographic works/videograms, see the International Federation of Phonogram and Videogram Producers (IFPI), *International Conventions and Copyright Regulations* (London: IFPI, 1985), Chart III.

60. *Convention Relating to the Distribution of Programme-Carrying Signals Transmitted by Satellite*, 1974, Article 2, item E2.
61. U.S. Copyright Office, *Intellectual Property Rights in World Commerce*, p. 64.
62. *Satellite Convention*, Article 4.
63. Office of Technology Assessment, *Intellectual Property Rights*, p. 244, n. 94.

9
CONCLUSIONS AND RECOMMENDATIONS

MATCHING STRATEGIES TO BARRIERS

In considering the effects that specific trade problems have on U.S. film and television producers, a useful division can be made between problems resulting from active practices of foreign governments and those that stem from a lack of activity on the part of overseas regimes. Active foreign government intervention is responsible for many of the trade restrictions historically faced by the industry, including screen quotas, import quotas, local work requirements, and restrictions on repatriation of film earnings.

Problems that arise from government inaction fall mainly under the heading of copyright infringement and include the toleration of unacceptable levels of print and signal theft, the presentation of unauthorized films, and piracy of videocassettes. Unlike screen quotas and other NTBs that are imposed directly by foreign governments, the infringement of copyrights is, for the most part, practiced by private individuals.[1] Such practices may be exacerbated by the lack of proper legal channels through which U.S. producers can raise issues of intellectual property theft. Alternatively, copyright infringement may result from the inadequate enforcement of existing copyright laws by foreign governments. From a trade negotiation standpoint, then, a foreign nation's agreement to increase protection of U.S. films is qualitatively different from an agreement to reduce or eliminate NTBs.

Our suggestion to disaggregate trade problems in this manner stems primarily from our belief that "active" and "passive" barriers will be perceived quite differently by trading parties as a result of the historical environment peculiar to the trade regimes where these issues are likely to be raised. In GATT, for example, the acceptance of certain "active" trade barriers in films has a long history, dating to the original adoption of film exceptions under Article IV. For this reason, industry efforts to reform existing GATT rules on film trade can claim an undeniable, historical legitimacy. By contrast, reform efforts that address passive government tolerance of video piracy in GATT will represent, in many ways, a sharp break with historical precedent. In addition, it must be recalled that the United States has begun to consider separate efforts to reform international copyright laws.[2] Without coordination, these efforts may overlap, and even undermine, industry support for intellectual property protection in GATT. This is not to say that parallel efforts should not continue. It is important to recognize, however, that U.S. positions on such issues as whether it should become a signatory to the Berne Convention will have repercussions in attempts to raise intellectual property concerns in GATT. Even U.S. efforts to *define* video piracy for inclusion in future GATT codes may face difficulties because of differences among nations' copyright laws.[3]

In a related vein, U.S. policymakers should not ignore the lessons learned from prior efforts to reform GATT. In particular, the codes negotiated in the Tokyo Round are quite instructive.[4] During that round, trade in services came to be recognized in the Agreement on Government Procurement and the Customs Valuation Agreement, albeit in a somewhat indirect manner. Services were included in these agreements because they could be characterized as adjunct features that primarily addressed trade in goods. This situation has parallels today. For example, it may be impossible to reach agreement on direct inclusion of video piracy in upcoming GATT negotiations. Yet U.S. policymakers may be able to structure agreements that safeguard industry "access" in overseas markets when legitimate business interests are at stake. If "access" is defined to include the activities that are necessary to minimize the effects of film piracy, then U.S. negotiators will have been partially successful, despite their failure to elevate intellectual property to formal treatment under GATT.

Like GATT, the OECD codes are a framework for negotiations that contains features that might be usefully adopted in a new trade-in-services regime. Unlike GATT, the OECD codes are not contractually binding. Accordingly, an OECD agreement can be viewed, in one sense, as an example of U.S. policy recommendations that differ dramatically from current practices under GATT. The OECD Code of Invisibles includes, in its film exception language, a qualification that may be very useful in a new agreement on films and television. Annex IV and Annex A allow the implementation of aids to film production "provided that they do not significantly distort international competition in export markets." This qualification represents a recognition of OECD countries that market impact may offset arguments for even "culturally" motivated trade barriers. The interdependence of motion picture demand in all channels of distribution exacerbates the harm done when barriers inhibit trade in any individual channel. For this reason, a standard of "significant distortion in international competition" might be used to foster an understanding of the interdependence and fragility of the motion picture industry among the trading parties. Moreover, given the increased importance of video piracy, the direct functional link between heightened trade barriers and increasing copyright infringement must be recognized. This interdependency might be acknowledged in future OECD codes or elsewhere through U.S. support for a "significant distortion" standard. Such a standard would comprehend the indirect effects that trade barriers have on the magnitude of film piracy. Here again, the OECD environment, which features nonbinding commitments by member countries, may provide an appropriate starting point.

While the distinction between active and passive trade barriers is valuable in the analysis of trade negotiation strategies for motion pictures, this does not mean that negotiations for their reduction should be conducted independently. The motion picture industry is characterized by numerous interdependencies throughout the release process that compound the problems

155

caused by video piracy. For this reason, the effects of any given NTB may differ considerably from country to country, depending on the degree of intellectual property protection afforded in each. For example, strict import quotas may be more damaging if they are imposed by a nation where cassette piracy is rampant. In this situation, the U.S. distributor may be hindered in his ability to respond to known piracy by increasing the available number of legitimate films in theatrical release or by accelerating a film's legal release into home video markets. The analytical disaggregation of barriers into active and passive categories may be viewed, however, as a framework for identifying conceptually distinct hindrances to trade and for formulating appropriate negotiating strategies.

THE MOST-FAVORED NATION PRINCIPLE

While an understanding of the historical environment of the various multinational trade regimes is important, a concern with historical precedent should not outweigh the need to reassess fundamental trade agreement concepts as they relate to trade in services today. In this regard, one of the most critical concepts that should be reviewed is the most-favored nation (MFN) principle of GATT.

The basic justification for the MFN principle is that non-discrimination among all trading parties is likely to lead to international "harmony" in the long run. However, strict adherence to such principles also means sacrificing opportunities to achieve workable liberalization on a bilateral or plurilateral basis in major markets. While the United States has sought to incorporate trade in services into a GATT-like forum for years, the trade agreements relating to services that have been reached to date in the Tokyo Round and elsewhere have been primarily code-conditional or bilateral in scope.[5] Moreover, the acceptance of unconditional MFN will signal the denigration of free trade as a principal U.S. negotiating objective for services. For these reasons, it appears disadvantageous for the United States to retain strong support for an unconditional MFN principle in services.

A code-conditional version appears more attractive. However, the principle may present one major disadvantage to the motion picture industry; most of the countries identified as important sources of pirated cassettes do not have significant domestic industries for film and television production or cinema exhibition.[6] Thus in these nations, legitimate film importers, local exhibitors, and others with an economic interest in reducing piracy of U.S. films do not constitute a powerful constituency in support of participation in a code-conditional film agreement. In addition, the production and sale of pirated cassettes may be a substantial local industry that has influence with the local government. Absent participation from these countries, it is possible that flows of pirated cassettes into signatory from nonsignatory countries may frustrate film agreements, even in those nations that have a large stake in the protection of intellectual property. In our view, however, this disadvantage does not offset the many practical advantages of code-conditional MFN. Rather, it speaks to the nature of the conditional agreement that should be negotiated, namely, one in which goods versus services trade-offs are encouraged.[7]

GOODS VS. SERVICES

Throughout this book, we have argued that the United States possesses a domestic opportunity advantage in the production and distribution of motion pictures and television programs. As a consequence, bilateral trade in video productions between the United States and other countries consists primarily of flows from the United States to its trading partners. The U.S. domestic opportunity advantage presents difficulties to negotiators who are trying to reduce barriers to film and television productions from the United States. The U.S. market is already open to imported films and television programs; therefore, reducing barriers to the American market is not a bargaining chip available to U.S. negotiators. It is true that consumers in countries that restrict the importation of foreign films and programs would be better off if these restrictions were eased, but consumer welfare alone has rarely proven to be a persuasive argument in trade negotiations. Finally, even if potential welfare gains were considerable, foreign officials are not likely to abandon longstanding concerns with the preservation of indigenous cultures and support for domestic producers.

We believe that American producers of video entertainment would benefit most from a bargaining position that facilitated the negotiation of the reduction of barriers in services in return for fewer restrictions on goods imported into the United States.[8] Such a negotiating position has several advantages. First, it correctly recognizes that different nations possess different comparative advantages—not only in the production of various goods but in services as well. Second, it introduces new voices of influence that provide incentives to persuade foreign policymakers to participate in code-conditional service agreements. Admittedly, opposing voices will surface as well. It is, however, the function of sovereign governments to facilitate such trade-offs as part of the political process. Moreover, recent legislation sanctioning the removal of General System of Preferences (GSP) benefits from countries that fail to protect intellectual property has already created implicit goods versus services trade-offs.[9] There has also been debate over the reduction of nontariff barriers in services that are ancillary to trade in goods. Thus the expansion and evolution of such trade-offs will probably continue, even if they are not proposed explicitly for service agreements in future GATT negotiations. We recommend, however, that U.S. negotiators in services consider a more explicit implementation of such trade-offs if meaningful gains are to be realized.

MARKET ACCESS, RIGHT OF ESTABLISHMENT, AND NATIONAL TREATMENT

In discussing right of establishment and the principle of national treatment for video products, it is important to distinguish between the application of these concepts to films and television programs and to the service of distributing films or programs. For films and television programs, access, national treatment, and right of establishment are conceptually distinct. For distribution services, however, access implies establishment. The principle of national treatment requires that there be no discrimination between imported goods or services and their domestic counterparts, once access to the domestic market has been achieved. This does not mean that market access is unrestricted; it means that a good or service that has cleared the barriers erected at the border will receive treatment within the country that is blind to national origin. For goods, national treatment implies access to national distribution systems on a par with domestically produced goods. For films and television programs, national treatment has the same implication. Right of establishment, if granted, goes beyond national treatment to permit foreign firms to establish operations in the host country. The general presumption has been, at least for goods, that national treatment provides foreign suppliers with adequate opportunity to exploit the commercial potential of their products once access has been granted. This presumption is generally not valid in the case of films and television programs.

Within the United States, films are released through a variety of distribution channels, including first-run cinemas, videocassettes, pay-per-view cable, pay cable, network television, independent television stations, second-run theaters, and drive-ins.[10] Other countries use a variety of distribution channels as well. As we pointed out in Chapter 7, close control over the sequence of release through different channels is essential to the maximization of film earnings within any given market. The sequencing of releases among national markets is also an important aspect of maximizing film earnings on a global basis. As with films, there is a well-defined release sequence for television programs that, for American productions, includes network television and releases for domestic and foreign syndication. For television programs, control over the temporal and geographic sequences of release is also important to the maximization of earnings.

For films and television programs, national treatment cannot provide the same degree of control over the sequencing of releases, among media and among countries, that can be achieved with such transnational distribution organizations as those that are maintained by the American majors in a number of countries. Because they do not internalize the economic effects of their actions on other markets, domestic distributors will not have the same incentives to control the "leakage" of products across national boundaries through piracy or untimely release to other media, such as broadcasting or cassettes, for which dissemination across national boundaries is hard to control. Furthermore, expertise and familiarity with films and television programs developed by an international organization are not easily passed on to domestic distributors. For these reasons, right of establishment is more important for the economic exploitation of imported video products than is generally the case for goods.

We recognize, however, that current U.S. negotiators have concluded that market access cannot be readily expanded into a negotiable right of "establishment."[11] Under the USTR's program, U.S. filmmakers would be guaranteed the limited right of "access" to the distribution systems of foreign firms, but they would not be guaranteed any general right to erect new establishments. Unfortunately, new or expanded points of presence by U.S. distributors may, in many instances, provide the only viable means of reacting to film piracy, particularly in smaller, low-income markets. In such markets, enforcement by government agencies will be effective only if scarce national resources can be diverted from other more pressing needs. Thus supplemental industry efforts almost certainly will be required to control piracy on an ongoing basis. In addition, through coordinated distribution overseas, U.S. distributors can adjust film and cassette release schedules in many countries, thereby reducing opportunities for "parallel imports" of pirated films or cassettes. This strategy would favor overall U.S. control of distribution in many markets as release patterns may require rapid adjustment to ensure the maximization of profits. Finally, to the extent that pay-per-view and pay-per-transaction modes of distribution supplement current forms of release, film distributors will, of necessity, become more involved in the day-to-day activities of cable companies and cassette distributors, irrespective of piracy considerations.[12]

Given these concerns, further discussions on the wisdom of excluding right of establishment from the current trade-in-services agenda is needed. One possible compromise might be the incorporation of a significant distortion standard that is comparable to that included in the film restrictions of the OECD's Code of Invisibles. Such a standard might be applied to "right of access" in the event that clear economic evidence demonstrates that local access alone cannot prevent large losses. New establishments may then be conditionally allowed by signatory nations. A conditional right would be particularly appropriate for those service industries, such as films, where the demarcation between trade and investment is not obvious.

OTHER CONCEPTS

The reliance on detailed procedures that set forth the rights and obligations of each party in the settlement of disputes is, in our view, another of the more important "features" that can be taken from GATT. While we have not assessed the applicability of the actual complaint practices (now used) in GATT,[13] we believe that an agreement to submit to a binding set of dispute-resolution procedures is essential for service trade liberalization. Indeed, the difficulties encountered in defining services trade for the reduction of nontariff barriers underscore the importance of creating a mechanism to address disputes in service industries.

The principle of transparency, which Senior Assistant Trade Representative Feketekuty has called the first principle to be followed in services trade, also seems to have value here. While we foresee negotiating problems based on the lack of willingness or ability of member governments to identify specific passive barriers, such as copyright infringement, we believe that adherence to the first principle is important if we are ever going to resolve trade-in-services disputes in an objective manner.

Finally, we support the U.S. government's efforts to extend GATT principles to state-run enterprises. In particular, it is our belief that government-supported monopsonies in the media industries protect local production at the expense of television and motion picture exporters from the United States and other countries. Because of interdependence in distribution, protectionism that is aimed at U.S. media products is also likely to increase the incidence of video piracy. Piracy, in turn, may undercut all legitimate video products, imported and domestic. For this reason, negotiated limits on foreign content quotas for government purchases of imported film and television programs may benefit all parties, including local media industries.

With respect to government-controlled monopolies in television and cable broadcasting, one further comment is in order. As we have observed, government monopolies may, through the exploitation of market power in purchasing, reduce the prices paid to both U.S. and domestic program producers. If prices are held below competitive levels, overall market size is reduced. This reduction in prices harms domestic producers disproportionately as potential earnings are reduced in the market where domestic producers have a native-language advantage over U.S. producers. Accordingly, it would appear that increased competition among foreign television and cable broadcasters would, in the long run, further the development of non-U.S. film and program production. Available evidence indicates that more competitive media markets, especially for television programming, would raise local producers' profits above the levels associated with sales to monopsonistic government broadcast agencies. Effective expansion of foreign markets for films and television programs by these means would also reduce, to some extent, the domestic opportunity advantage of the American film and television industries.

For U.S. policymakers, this line of reasoning suggests a further response to nations that would impose culturally based "exceptions" on trade agreements in video products. For those nations, we recommend a reexamination of the television program purchase decisions that affect U.S. *and native* producers. When purchase prices appear lower than prices in more competitive broadcast markets, U.S. producers' interests may coincide with the interests of foreign producers who would benefit from more competitive markets for programming. In this way, new alliances might be formed within the media sectors of trading nations, and new voices might be heard in support of trade liberalization.

CULTURE, INTELLECTUAL PROPERTY, AND TRADE REFORM

It is, of course, impossible to estimate, or even to define precisely, the value of cultural preservation to a sovereign nation. For this reason, cultural differences and their importance to national identity cannot be readily incorporated into a framework for analyzing barriers to trade in films and programs. However, foreign taxpayers should recognize the cost of fostering and maintaining a major domestic film industry in the face of the domestic opportunity advantage enjoyed by producers from the United States and other English-language countries—an advantage that is exacerbated by policies that hinder the commercial development of indigenous media industries. This cost is likely to be both substantial and continuing as the size of the large and wealthy English-speaking population is not likely to decline. With widespread recognition of this truth, it is our hope that a more rational emphasis on worldwide market efficiencies can be introduced and that trade liberalization in films and programming can proceed in a more enlightened, and perhaps somewhat less emotional, manner.

It is likely that some culturally based discrimination will always remain. There will probably be some countries that, while recognizing the full costs of aiding their domestic film industries, will still elect to provide help in some form. Nevertheless, as we have seen, theft of the artistic content of films and programs is common throughout the world. The contradiction between the claims of cultural preservation and the tolerance of intellectual property theft is plain. Theft of intellectual property harms all cultural expression and is antithetical to any true affirmation of national pride. For this reason, there can be no real defense for a nation's tolerance of film piracy on cultural grounds, although for the poorest nations, scarcity of resources obviously affects the level of enforcement that can be achieved. Subsidies to a domestic industry are less disruptive of market processes and allow for greater consumer choice than the protectionist measures that are usually employed. Subsidies also have the advantage of revealing the true costs of aid to an industry.

We recommend that U.S. policymakers incorporate issues of intellectual property into emerging trade regimes. We also recommend that they resist efforts to subject intellectual property reform to the "culturally" motivated exceptions and derogations so common in existing trade agreements on motion pictures. Specifically, we recommend that the United States move to:

> Establish worldwide cooperation in identifying and reducing trade barriers in video products wherever they exist;

> Establish intellectual property theft and copyright infringement as barriers to trade to be remedied under GATT or a new regime governing trade in service;

> Establish a foreign corporation's right to respond to intellectual piracy and copyright infringement through access to local law enforcement authorities as well as through multinational trade forums;

> Resolve disputes that result from differences in copyright law among nations through formal disputeresolution procedures in GATT; and

> Allow market access and conditional right of establishment as needed to respond to intellectual property theft and to exploit commercial opportunities.

NOTES

1. In certain instances, allegations of complicity in film piracy schemes have been levied against government employees directly.

For example, industry sources have charged that in the Philippines, lengthy customs procedures allow for the unauthorized replication of U.S. film prints by Philippine pirates who can obtain prints during the customs review process.

2. See, for example, recommendations of the United States Copyright Office, in *To Secure Intellectual Property Rights in World Commerce*, September 21, 1984, pp. 151–69.

3. In this regard, the Geneva Phonograms Convention's provision concerning record piracy may be useful since it specifies that many types of domestic laws, including laws relating to unfair competition, may be used to prosecute audio pirates in a foreign market.

4. William Diebold and Helena Stalson have argued that even the process of negotiating trade-in-services agreements on NTBs will more resemble negotiations on NTBs in goods during the Tokyo Rounds than earlier rounds of GATT tariff reduction. See William Diebold and Helena Stalson, "Negotiating Issues in International Services Transaction," in *Trade Policy in the 1980s*, chapter 17, ed. William R. Cline (Cambridge, Mass. MIT Press, 1983), p. 591.

5. Assistant U.S. Trade Representative Geza Feketekuty has praised the recent U.S.-Israeli agreement on services as both "comprehensive" and instructive.

6. Saudi Arabia, an important source of pirate cassettes in Europe and the Middle East, is an example. According to the U.S. Copyright Office, virtually the entire domestic market for videocassettes of motion pictures in Saudi Arabia is served by pirates. Yet, legitimate releases of most U.S. films are banned in Saudi Arabia for religious reasons, and there is very little domestic production.

7. For the poorest countries, it is likely that the effective enforcement of intellectual property laws can never become a primary government objective because of competitive demands on scarce resources. Thus participation in an unconditional MFN agreement would be ineffective and would seem to require supplemental direct action by U.S. film distributors to a degree comparable to that necessary under a conditional code.

8. Diebold and Stalson have written that "if it is true, as is often said, that the decline of American competitiveness in many branches of manufacturing is offset by a gain in competitiveness in many services (plainly not all), then the United States should be especially interested in bargains that reduce foreign restrictions

165

on services and may have to offer easier access to domestic markets for some products in return," "Negotiating Issues in International Services Transactions," p. 613.

9. The GSP Removal Act specifically allows the U.S. president to withdraw GSP benefits from any country that fails to provide "adequate and effective means under its laws for foreign nations to secure, to exercise, and to enforce exclusive rights in intellectual property, including patents, trademarks and copyrights."

10. See David Waterman, "Prerecorded Home Video and the Distribution of Theatrical Feature Films," in *Video Media Competition*, ed. Eli M. Noam (New York: Columbia University Press, 1985), pp. 221–43.

11. The U.S. position is essentially that since issues on rights of establishment have proved intractable in all GATT negotiations to date regarding goods, the same difficulties would be encountered in services.

12. Pay-per-transaction has been proposed by Ron Berger, president of National Video Inc., as a means by which studios can share in cassette rentals on a per-transaction basis. See James Melanson, "Majors to Share Video Returns," *Variety*, January 6, 1986, p. 1.

13. As we have mentioned in earlier chapters, a recent survey of the effectiveness of dispute resolution procedures under GATT by the U.S. International Trade Commission was reasonably sanguine as to the effectiveness of these procedures. See U.S. International Trade Commission, *Review of the Effectiveness of Trade Dispute Settlements Under the GATT and the Tokyo Round Agreements*, Report to the Committee on Finance, U.S. Senate Investigation, No. 332-212, U.S. ITC Publication 1793, December 1985.

APPENDIXES

A

FILM IMPORT AND PRODUCTION STATISTICS FOR NINETY-TWO COUNTRIES

O ur objective in constructing Table A–1 was to provide a comparison of film import numbers and domestic production statistics, using the most recent data reported by UNESCO, for each country or territory. The twin objectives of using the most recent data and matching the years for production and import statistics were not always simultaneously achievable. For the majority of cases where import and production statistics were available for the same year, data for the most recent year were used in constructing the table. For countries or territories for which UNESCO reported both import and production statistics, but for different years, data were selected to minimize the difference between the years for the two sets of annual statistics. If only import or export statistics were provided, the most recent data were always employed.

Table A–1. Film Production and Imports.

Country	Production Year	Production Number	Imports Year	Imports Number	Production/ Production + Imports
Africa					
Algeria	1983	10(3)[e]	1983	135	0.07
Angola	a	a	1979	186	a
Cameroon	1975	1	b	b	b
Egypt[d]	1975	90	1978	385	0.19
Ethiopia	a	a	1981	211	a
Ghana	1975	1	1980	24	0.04
Ivory Coast	a	a	1979	595	a
Libyan Arab Jamahiriya	1975	3(1)[e]	1978	180	0.02
Mauritania	a	a	1981	190	a
Mauritius	a	a	1983	321	a
Morocco	1983	12	1983	302	0.04
Mozambique	a	a	1983	68	a
Nigeria	1980	40(20)[e]	1979	105	0.28
Rwanda	a	a	1981	164	a
Somalia	a	a	1983	449	a
Sudan	1983	2(1)[e]	1982	137	0.01
United Republic of Tanzania	a	a	1981	162	a
North America					
Bermuda	a	a	1981	122	a
Canada	1980	32	1980	777	0.04
Cuba	1983	9(1)[e]	1983	133	0.06
Grenada	a	a	1979	50	a
Guatemala	a	a	1983	296	a
Haiti	a	a	1981	422	a
Mexico	1983	113(8)[e]	1983	309	0.27
Nicaragua	a	a	1981	231	a
Trinidad and Tobago	a	a	1978	401	a
United States[d]	1983	396	b	b	b
South America					
Argentina	1983	16(1)[e]	1983	205	0.07
Bolivia	a	a	1979	394	a
Brazil	1980	103	1980	497	0.17
Colombia	1983	0	1983	363	0.00
Guyana	1975	4	1980	497	0.01
Peru	1980	2(1)[e]	1980	682	0.00
Venezuela	1980	16(4)[e]	1980	904	0.02

United States	France	Italy	India	USSR	United Kingdom	Federal Republic of Germany	Japan	Hong Kong	Other Countries
46.7	4.4	2.2	22.2	3.0	2.2	0.7	c	c	18.5
15.1	18.3	9.1	1.1	14.0	11.3	1.6	2.2	c	27.4
b	b	b	b	b	b	b	b	b	b
51.7	1.0	19.2	0.3	6.8	4.7	0.3	3.1	4.2	8.8
60.7	1.4	6.2	9.0	17.1	c	c	c	0.5	5.2
12.5	c	4.2	c	c	c	c	c	83.3	c
31.3	34.8	11.1	8.2	f	c	c	f	f	14.6
38.9	c	9.4	9.4	3.3	10.6	c	0.6	2.8	25.0
31.6	21.1	5.3	42.1	c	c	c	c	c	c
c	78.5	c	21.5	c	c	c	c	c	c
21.2	17.2	9.3	18.9	2.0	7.9	1.0	2.6	15.9	4.0
7.4	2.9	10.3	c	16.2	4.4	c	27.9	c	30.9
100.0	c	c	c	c	c	c	c	c	c
22.6	7.9	2.4	32.9	c	c	c	c	6.1	28.0
c	c	74.4	25.6	c	c	c	c	c	c
18.2	7.3	3.6	25.5	7.3	10.9	3.6	c	7.3	16.1
32.7	1.2	11.1	32.1	8.0	4.9	0.6	1.2	8.0	c
79.5	1.6	c	c	c	9.0	c	c	8.2	1.6
38.0	13.1	11.7	10.7	f	1.7	2.3	f	14.5	8.0
10.5	6.0	6.0	c	12.0	4.5	3.0	6.8	c	51.1
16.0	6.0	c	c	c	24.0	c	20.0	34.0	c
45.6	2.4	11.1	c	c	4.1	0.7	c	c	36.1
40.8	41.5	0.7	c	c	1.9	c	c	10.0	5.2
53.7	5.5	5.5	c	1.0	6.5	2.6	1.9	3.9	19.4
68.8	1.7	5.2	c	0.4	3.0	c	c	2.2	18.6
50.4	1.5	6.0	16.5	c	4.5	0.2	c	c	20.9
b	b	b	b	b	b	b	b	b	b
51.2	5.9	18.5	0.5	1.5	2.4	3.4	1.5	c	15.1
44.4	3.6	16.2	0.5	3.6	4.6	1.5	1.3	2.8	21.6
42.3	3.4	26.6	c	0.2	1.8	4.0	3.8	13.1	4.8
46.3	2.8	9.1	c	0.3	2.8	0.3	1.4	1.7	35.5
72.4	c	c	14.5	c	c	c	c	13.1	c
43.7	4.7	19.2	2.5	1.5	2.1	3.2	0.7	1.8	20.7
38.3	6.6	16.3	c	2.0	c	2.4	1.4	8.7	24.2

Sources of Imported Films (percent)

Table A–1   continued.

Country	Production Year	Production Number	Imports Year	Imports Number	Production/ Production + Imports
Asia					
Afghanistan	1980	2	1979	41	0.05
Brunei Darussalam	1970	6	1980	395	0.01
Hong Kong	1983	118(2)e	1983	429	0.22
India	1980	742	1980	119	0.86
Indonesia	1983	77(1)e	1983	212	0.27
Iran, Islamic Republic of	1983	24	1983	96	0.20
Iraq	1980	2	1980	186	0.01
Israel	1983	17	1983	267	0.06
Japan	1980	321(1)e	1980	209	0.61
Jordan	aa	a	1983	438	a
Korea, Republic of	1983	96(5)e	1983	26	0.79
Kuwait	a	a	1983	150	a
Lao People's Democratic Republic	a	a	1981	78	a
Malaysia	1983	13	1983	1045	0.01
Maldives	a	a	1983	49	a
Pakistan	1983	84(2)e	1983	81	0.51
Philippines	1975	143	1980	b	b
Qatar	1975	1	1980	1140	0.00
Singapore	1983	0	1983	533	0.00
Sri Lanka	1983	33	1983	151	0.18
Syrian Arab Republic	1983	24	1983	149	0.14
Thailand	1975	55	1978	401	0.12
Turkey	1983	72	1981	208	0.26
Vietnam	1975	7	1978	207	0.03
Yemen	a	a	1981	174	a
Europe					
Albania	1983	14	1983	7	0.67
Austria	1983	23(7)e	1983	314	0.07
Belgium	1983	21(7)e	b	b	b
Bulgaria	1983	32	1983	164	0.16
Czechoslovakiad	1983	53(8)e	1983	177	0.23
Denmark	1983	11	1983	233	0.05
Finland	1983	13	1983	212	0.06
France	1983	161(30)e	1983	241	0.40
German Democratic Republic	1983	16	1983	118	0.12
Germany, Federal Republic of	1983	91(8)e	1983	322	0.22
Gibraltard	a	a	1981	369	a
Greece	1983	47	1983	261	0.15

	Sources of Imported Films (percent)								
United States	France	Italy	India	USSR	United Kingdom	Federal Republic of Germany	Japan	Hong Kong	Other Countries
f	f	f	2.4	85.4	f	f	c	c	12.2
32.4	c	c	c	c	0.8	c	c	45.6	21.3
28.4	5.1	6.8	0.7	0.5	4.9	7.7	8.2	c	37.8
21.1	0.8	0.8	c	13.4	8.4	c	0.8	0.8	53.8
34.0	2.3	6.1	10.4	c	5.7	0.5	1.4	30.7	8.9
13.5	2.1	22.9	c	26.0	10.4	c	2.1	c	22.9
22.0	10.2	8.6	10.8	3.2	21.5	0.5	c	c	23.1
44.6	8.2	8.6	c	2.2	6.7	2.6	2.2	0.4	24.3
67.5	12.0	5.3	c	1.4	4.8	1.4	c	2.9	4.8
30.8	1.1	19.4	11.4	c	0.7	c	c	6.8	29.7
61.5	3.8	7.7	c	c	3.8	3.8	c	11.5	7.7
c	c	21.3	56.7	c	c	2.0	6.7	13.3	c
c	c	c	23.1	60.3	c	c	c	c	16.7
22.3	1.3	3.5	11.9	0.3	6.5	2.0	2.6	36.6	13.0
8.2	2.0	c	85.7	2.0	c	c	c	c	2.0
b	b	b	b	b	b	b	b	b	b
45.1	c	0.7	c	c	11.0	0.5	0.4	39.0	3.2
13.2	0.6	7.9	48.2	c	0.5	0.3	c	3.9	25.4
34.7	1.7	5.1	12.8	c	4.1	3.0	1.7	26.1	10.9
48.3	c	0.7	18.5	0.7	27.8	0.7	c	2.6	0.7
c	c	c	8.7	5.4	19.5	c	c	c	66.4
42.1	f	5.2	3.5	f	1.0	f	3.2	40.1	4.7
55.8	8.7	15.9	0.5	3.8	2.9	5.8	c	5.3	1.4
c	c	c	c	43.5	c	c	c	c	56.5
28.7	2.9	5.7	20.1	5.7	4.0	2.9	4.0	2.9	23.0
c	28.6	14.3	c	c	14.3	14.3	28.6	c	c
36.0	14.6	13.7	c	0.6	3.5	12.7	c	1.3	17.5
b	b	b	b	b	b	b	b	b	b
7.9	4.3	3.0	1.8	32.3	c	0.6	3.0	c	47.0
10.2	9.0	3.4	c	22.0	2.8	3.4	c	c	49.2
51.1	6.9	7.7	c	0.4	7.3	7.7	0.4	3.0	15.5
48.6	3.8	4.7	c	7.1	3.8	2.4	0.9	c	28.8
44.0	c	14.1	4.6	1.7	7.9	5.8	2.1	14.9	5.0
5.9	5.1	2.5	c	30.5	c	6.8	2.5	c	46.6
34.2	8.1	12.7	c	0.3	4.7	c	0.3	1.6	38.2
89.7	c	c	c	c	f	1.9	c	c	8.4
39.1	14.6	18.4	c	0.8	5.4	8.8	0.4	3.4	9.2

Table A–1 continued.

Country	Production Year	Production Number	Imports Year	Imports Number	Production/ Production + Imports
Hungary	1983	27(2)ᵉ	1983	198	0.12
Iceland	1983	4	b	b	b
Ireland	1980	0	1980	214	0.00
Italy	1983	140(12)ᵉ	1983	275	0.34
Netherlands	1980	7	1980	329	0.02
Norway	1983	8	1983	284	0.03
Poland	1983	36(1)ᵉ	1983	90	0.29
Portugal	1980	10(1)ᵉ	1980	386	0.03
Romania	1983	33(1)ᵉ	1983	113	0.23
San Marino	a	a	1983	314	a
Spain	1983	99	1981	463	0.18
Sweden	1980	20(3)ᵉ	1979	318	0.06
Switzerland	1983	28(6)ᵉ	1983	466	0.06
United Kingdom	1983	39	1983	265	0.13
Yugoslavia	1983	31(2)ᵉ	1983	187	0.14
Oceania					
Australia	1983	10	1983	900	0.01
New Zealand	a	a	1979	564	a
Norfolk Island	a	a	1979	120	a
Tonga	a	a	1979	421	a
Vanuatu	a	a	1981	207	a
USSR	1983	162(6)ᵉ	1977	147	0.52

Sources: UNESCO, Statistical Yearbook, (Paris: UNESCO, 1984), Table 8.2; UNESCO, Statistical Yearbook (Paris: UNESCO, 1985), Tables 9.1 and 9.2.

a. No production data provided.

b. No import data provided.

c. Negligible quantity.

d. MPAA is UNESCO's source.

e. Number in parentheses is coproductions with another country that have been counted as part of the total productions number.

f. Due to imprecision in the data, films from this country may have been included in the "other countries" category.

Sources of Imported Films (percent)									
United States	France	Italy	India	USSR	United Kingdom	Federal Republic of Germany	Japan	Hong Kong	Other Countries
20.2	9.6	6.6	5.6	19.7	3.0	5.1	0.5	c	29.8
b	b	b	b	b	b	b	b	b	b
51.9	1.7	3.8	c	c	30.2	1.7	0.4	1.7	8.5
45.1	24.0	c	c	5.5	5.8	8.4	c	1.1	10.2
42.9	16.7	7.9	c	1.8	6.1	8.2	1.5	6.4	8.5
51.4	10.9	7.0	c	1.1	9.5	3.5	1.1	c	15.5
11.1	3.3	2.2	c	40.0	1.1	1.1	c	c	41.1
33.9	15.3	17.1	7.0	c	14.8	2.1	1.8	4.4	3.6
5.3	3.5	2.7	c	38.9	1.8	c	c	c	47.8
31.2	12.4	39.2	c	1.0	7.3	3.5	0.3	1.3	3.8
40.6	7.1	16.2	c	1.7	8.4	7.3	0.4	2.2	16.0
52.5	14.2	6.0	c	2.8	7.2	4.7	c	c	12.6
40.6	21.7	7.9	1.3	0.4	4.3	11.4	5.4	2.8	6.4
54.7	f	f	f	f	c	f	f	f	45.3
35.3	8.0	10.7	—	8.0	7.0	4.8	1.1	7.5	26.2
37.0	5.2	3.9	0.3	2.2	5.8	4.3	1.3	17.9	22.0
49.1	9.6	3.7	0.2	1.1	13.3	6.9	1.6	2.5	12.1
60.0	c	c	c	c	40.0	c	c	c	c
45.1	c	f	c	f	f	c	f	45.1	9.7
18.4	39.6	8.2	c	c	8.2	11.1	3.9	10.6	c
10.2	8.2	4.1	f	c	2.7	f	f	f	74.8

A MODEL OF TRADE IN FILMS
AND TELEVISION PROGRAMS

In Chapter 4 we presented an analysis of the economics of international competition in films and television. There we argued that the dominance of American films in foreign markets is explained by the large English-language market in combination with the natural advantage that domestic films enjoy when competing with foreign language products. The results of that analysis formed the basis for most of the subsequent arguments underlying our policy recommendations. The analysis of Chapter 4 was largely verbal, and illustrative examples were provided. While we think that the argument is intuitively appealing, we also recognize that the complexities of market interactions sometimes prove initial intuitions to be an unreliable guide. Furthermore, even when initial intuition is proven correct, a formal statement of the problem often produces additional insight and, at the very least, increases one's confidence in initial results. In this appendix we formally develop the model that was presented verbally in the text. The model is sufficiently general to be applicable to either the film or the television program industry without changing either the notation or the basic structure of the model. For expositional convenience, the model is presented as an analysis of trade in films. The fact that the model could have been presented as an analysis of trade in television programs should be kept in mind.

To simplify the analysis, we assume that all firms are integrated producer-distributors that handle only one film at any given time. We also assume that total film industry revenues are fixed for each country and that producers compete for revenue shares. Because consumers have varied tastes in films, and because uncertainties are inherent in the production of films, no two films are perfect substitutes. However, the audience appeal of a film is determined in part by the quality of the inputs (actors, scriptwriters, special effects, etc.) employed in its production. Therefore a filmmaker can increase his expected share of film revenues by increasing his expenditure on inputs relative to other filmmakers by, for example, hiring more famous actors and directors with better track records.

We assume that the industry is competitive. This implies that if, on average, filmmakers earn supracompetitive returns on films, new filmmakers will enter the business. New entry reduces the average expected revenue per film, until the expected returns on film investments fall to competitive levels. The model assumes a two-country world (although one of the countries could represent the domestic market and the other country the rest of the world).

We will call the two countries A and B. Variables for Country A filmmakers are identified by subscript i and for Country B filmmakers by subscript j where $i = 1, \ldots Na$, and $j = 1, \ldots, Nb$, Na and Nb being the number of filmmakers in Countries A and B, respectively. We assume symmetry for all filmmakers in a given country. Thus we can conduct much of the analysis in terms of a representative filmmaker for each country. Define Sia and Sib as the shares of a representative Country A filmmaker of market revenue in Countries A and B, respectively. Similarly, let Sja and Sjb be the shares of a representative Country B filmmaker of market revenue in Countries A and B. Ei (Ej) is defined to be the expenditures of a Country A (B) filmmaker on inputs, which we will refer to as creative inputs, that increase the expected audience appeal of a film. For a larger budget, a producer can employ talent associated with greater box office success in the past, which would be expected to make a larger contribution to the current project. The level of these expenditures is a matter of choice to the filmmaker. In addition, we assume that filmmakers must incur other costs, represented by K, that are fixed in magnitude, say, to maintain a distribution network of a size adequate to make commercial success possible.

Different languages are spoken in A and B, and the inhabitants of each country are unable to understand the spoken language of the other. Therefore films produced in the language of Country A must be either subtitled or dubbed in the language of B to be shown in Country B, and films produced in Country B must be given similar treatment before they can be shown in Country A. Other things equal, inhabitants of both countries prefer pictures filmed in their own language to dubbed or subtitled foreign-language films. Therefore the existence of different national languages is a source of advantage to film-makers competing in their own market and a disadvantage when competing in the foreign market.

Assume that foreign films in competition with domestic films in both countries have a handicap of h ($h < 1$), such that foreign films can expect audiences h times as large as the audiences of domestically produced films with the same budget, and let the Si's and Sj's be determined by Ei, Ej, Na, and Nb, according to the following formulas:

$$Sia = Ei/(NaEi + hNbEj),$$

$$Sib = hEi/(hNaEi + NbEj),$$

$$Sja = hEj/(NaEi + hNbEj),$$

$$Sjb = Ej/(hNaEi + NbEj).$$

Define Ra and Rb to be total film revenues in Countries A and B,[1] respectively and let Pi be the profits of the ith filmmaker in Country A and $P'i$ be the derivative of the ith filmmaker's profits with respect to its own expenditures on creative inputs. Pj and $P'j$ are defined similarly for the ith filmmaker in B. Equilibrium is described by the following four equations, where Ra and Rb are taken to be constants.

$$Pi = RaSia + RbSib - Ei - K = 0. \tag{B.1}$$

$$P'i = RaS'ia + RbS'ib - 1 = 0. \tag{B.2}$$

$$Pj = RaSja + RbSjb - Ej - K = 0. \tag{B.3}$$

$$P'j = RaS'ja + RbS'jb - 1 = 0. \tag{B.4}$$

S'ia and *S'ib* are the partial derivatives of the market shares of a Country A filmmaker with respect to *its own* expenditure on creative inputs. *S'ja* and *S'jb* are defined analogously for a Country B filmmaker.

To keep the analysis manageable, we assume that $Ra = Rb = R$ initially. If other economic variables are the same in both countries, we will also observe $Ei = Ej$ and $Na = Nb$. We will take this as our starting point and then examine the consequences of introducing variation in the exogenous variables, market revenues, language handicap, and fixed costs for the number of producers and expenditures on creative inputs for each country.

As long as we assume that Ra is equal to Rb, Equation (B.1) is identical to Equation (B.3), and Equation (B.2) is identical to Equation (B.4), except that the subscripts refer to different countries. Therefore, as long as we are not concerned with the effects of differences in the sizes of the different markets, we can work with (B.1) and (B.2) [or (B.3) and (B.4)] as a two-equation system. Suppressing subscripts and solving (B.1) and (B.2) simultaneously for N (the common value for Na and Nb), we get

$$N = [R(1 + h^2) / (1 + h)^2 K]^{1/2}.$$

It is immediately obvious that N increases with R and decreases with K. These are both intuitive results. If fixed costs increase, there is less "room" in the industry, while the market will support more films if revenue increases. Differentiating the expression for N with respect to h, we get

$$dN / dh = 2K R (h^2 - 1) / (1 + h)^4 K^2 < 0.$$

So linguistic barriers between markets increase the total number of producers. Let E be the common value for Ei and Ej. The equilibrium value for E is

$$E = [RK (1 + h)^2 / (1 + h^2)]^{1/2} - K.$$

E obviously increases in R. If the markets increase in size, more expensive films will be produced. The effect of changes in K on production budgets is less obvious. Differentiating E with respect to K, we get

$$dE / dK = \{[(R/K) (1 + h)^2 / (1 + h^2)]^{1/2} - 1\} / 2.$$

This is positive as long as $R > 4K$. Since revenues must at least cover fixed costs, increasing fixed costs results in larger production budgets, as long as there are at least two producers in each market. The intuition underlying this result is that while an increase in fixed costs reduces the number of producers that may exist in a market in equilibrium, reducing the number of producers means that the revenue to be shared by the remaining producers has increased. The surviving producers will compete by spending more on production budgets in an attempt to increase their shares of a revenue pie that is now divided into fewer pieces. The fact that per producer revenues are increased by reducing the number of producers means that the effect is the same as if revenues had been increased through an increase in the market.

It is worth noting that these results for the completely symmetric two-country case also hold for a single country. If h is set equal to 1, then (B.1) and (B.2) may be thought of as describing a single country with $2N$ firms. This provides a basis for understanding the intuition for the results derived through simulation for the two-country case below, where we explore the effects of changing the relative sizes of the countries. As we have just shown, without trade, production budgets will be higher in larger markets, and larger markets will also support more producers. If production budgets are higher in the larger market, then films from the larger market should do better in the smaller country than the smaller country's films will do in the larger country.

To examine the consequences for Ei, Ej, Na, and Nb of a difference in the sizes of the national markets, we differentiate totally Equations (B.1) through (B.4) with respect to Ra. This gives us four equations that are linear in dEi / dRa, dEj / dRa, dNa / dRa, and dNb / dRb, the variables of interest. Stated in matrix form, we have $Adr = Br$, where

A is the 4×4 matrix of partial derivatives,[2]

$$
A = \begin{vmatrix}
\partial Pi/\partial Ei & \partial Pi/\partial Na & \partial Pi/\partial Ej & \partial Pi/\partial Nb \\
\partial P'i/\partial Ei & \partial P'i/\partial Na & \partial P'i/\partial Ej & \partial P'i/\partial Nb \\
\\
\partial Pj/\partial Ei & \partial Pj/\partial Na & \partial Pj/\partial Ej & \partial Pj/\partial Nb \\
\partial P'j/\partial Ei & \partial P'j/\partial Na & \partial P'j/\partial Ej & \partial P'j/\partial Nb
\end{vmatrix}
$$

and Dr and Br are 4×1 column vectors,

$$
Dr = \begin{vmatrix}
dEi/dRa \\
dNa/dRa \\
\\
dEj/dRa \\
dNb/dRa
\end{vmatrix}
\quad \text{and } Br = \begin{vmatrix}
\partial Pi/\partial Ra \\
\partial P'i/\partial Ra \\
\\
\partial Pj/\partial Ra \\
\partial P'j/\partial Ra
\end{vmatrix}
$$

For given initial values of K, h, and R, the values of the elements of A and Br are easily calculated. Therefore the values of the elements of Dr can be determined with the usual matrix techniques. For $K = 10$, $h = .9$, and $Ra = Rb = 1{,}000$ initially, we have

$$
A = \begin{vmatrix}
-0.4634 & -10 & -0.5366 & -9.9448 \\
-0.0041 & -0.0649 & -0.0035 & -0.065 \\
\\
-0.5366 & -9.9448 & -0.4634 & -10 \\
-0.0035 & -0.0651 & -0.0041 & -0.0649
\end{vmatrix}
$$

$$
1000 \times Br = \begin{vmatrix}
-74.3294 \\
-\ 0.5423 \\
\\
-66.8965 \\
-\ 0.4757
\end{vmatrix}
\quad \text{and } Dr = \begin{vmatrix}
0.040 \\
0.075 \\
\\
0.032 \\
-0.071
\end{vmatrix}
$$

So increasing the size of the market in Country A leads to an increase in the quality (we are using quality synonomously with audience appeal) and number of films produced in Country A. The quality of films increases in Country B, but not by as much as in A, and the number of films produced in B declines. For the larger country, the size of the domestic market is a source of competitive advantage.

NOTES

1. *Ra* and *Rb* would be defined as television industry revenues if the model were applied to trade in television programs.
2. Note that these are partial derivatives with respect to representative Ei and Ej. This contrasts with the S' expressions, which are partials with respect to expenditure on creative inputs for a single firm.

Index

Admission prices, 4
Admission taxes, 108, 109, 125
Advertising regulations, 54–55, 139–140
Advertising sales versus government
    funding, 91–95
Affordability explanation, 63, 66
Africa, 18
Agreement on Government Procurement,
    133, 154
Agreement on Technical Barriers to
    Trade, 133
Algeria, 111
American Enterprise Institute for Public
    Research (AEI), 2
American Film Marketing Association
    (AFMA), 32–33
Anguilla, 104
Anticompetitive acts, 63, 65, 146
Antigua, 104
Antola, L., 96
Approximation principle, 140
Arabic language market, 18, 41, 52, 87,
    88, 112
ARABSAT, 52
Argentina, 102, 110
    film attendance and revenues, 21
    local work requirements, 108
    quantitative restrictions, 105–106, 113
    subsidies, 109
    television exports, 46
Aruba, 104
Asia, 40
Attendance figures, 18–19
Australia, 16, 87
    private, commercial broadcast systems,
        50, 95
    subsidies, 137

trade barriers, 103, 106, 111
Austria, 102, 103, 109

Bahamas, 104
Bahrain, 115 n.6
Barbados, 104
Belgium, 52, 54, 109, 110
Benelux countries, 53
Berger, Ron, 166, n.12
Bermuda, 104
Berne Convention, 10, 142–154
Bolivia, 110
Box office taxes, 109, 121
Brazil, 108, 109, 111
    quantitative restrictions, 105, 113
    television programming, 41, 44, 46, 95,
        96–97
    video piracy, 103, 115 n.6
Broadcast signals, theft of, 104–105,
    146–147
Brussels Satellite Convention (1974), 145,
    146–147
Burma, 111
Burundi, 106, 110

Cable News Network (CNN), 46
Cable television, 41, 46, 53–55, 104–105,
    137
Cameroon, 106, 110
Canada, 89
    cable television, 95, 105
    private, commercial television
        broadcast systems, 50, 95
    trade barriers, 103, 106, 109, 111, 112,
        115–116
Canadian Broadcast Company, 106
Canadian Film Industry Task Force, 112

Capital movement, 131, 134, 135
Caribbean Basin countries, 104
Carmen, 24
CBS survey, 102, 104, 106, 111
Censorship, 117–118, 120
China, People's Republic of, 97 n.3, 111
China, Republic of (Taiwan), 106–107, 108, 109, 110, 113–114
CIC, 20
Clockwork Orange, 21
Code of Invisibles, 134, 136–137, 155, 161
Code of Liberalization of Capital Movements, 134, 135
Coditel case, 144–145
Colombia, 103, 105, 106, 110
Colonialism, 87
Columbia, 20
Comedy programs, televised, 46
Commission of the European Community, 24–25, 137
Comparative advantage, theory of, 62, 80 n.2, 119, 158
Competitive advantage, 63, 65, 146
Compulsory licensing, 138, 143–144
Copyright protection, 99–105, 117, 122, 123–124, 125, 153
  Berne/UCC Agreements, 142–144
  cross-border television, 54, 138
  distinction between services and goods, 144
Court of Justice, 139–140, 144
Customs Valuation Agreement, 133, 154
"Dallas," 138
Debauve case, 139–140
Denmark, 109
Diebold, William, 165 n.4, 165–166 n.8
Direct broadcast satellites (DBS), 50, 53
Direct investment, 131, 135, 155
Discriminatory taxes, 108–109, 115–116 n.12
Distortion standard, 155, 161
Distribution subsidiaries, 112, 113–114, 121
Domestic opportunity advantage (DOA), 9, 10, 68, 119, 157
Dominican Republic, 104
Dramatic series, televised, 46
Dubbing, 9, 108, 111–112, 121

Earnings remittance restrictions, 110–114
Eastern Europe, 18, 41, 49, 111
Economic model, 8, 61–82, 177–183
Economic regulation, theories of, 118–119
Ecuador, 4
Egypt: motion picture industry, 18, 87, 88
  television industry, 41
  trade barriers, 105, 106, 110, 111, 112, 113
El Norte, 23–24
El Salvador, 110
English-language market, 8–9, 25–26, 66, 85, 86–87
Entertainment programs, televised, 46
Entre Nous, 24
E.T., 21, 24
European Economic Community (EEC), 10, 55
  copyright provisions, 144–145
  Green Paper, 137–139, 144–145
  trade agreements, 137–140
  trade barriers, 103–104, 105, 106, 108, 113
European Parliament's Committee on Youth, Culture, Education, Information and Sport, 140
European Space Agency (ESA), 52
Eurovision, 41

Feketekuty, Geza, 132, 161
Film distributors (U.S.), 36 n.10
Film import and production statistics, 169–175
Film rental regulations, 110, 114
Film screen quotas, 136
Film taxes, 108–109
Filmmakers, independent, (U.S.), 32–33, 36 n.12
Films, foreign: U.S. market, 8, 22–26
Finland, 94, 109, 110
Foreign investment barriers, 131, 135, 155
France, 65, 87, 102, 106, 109
  attendance figures, 18
  Centre National de Las Cinematographie, 110
  film rental terms, 110, 114

local work requirements, 108
motion picture industry, 17, 84–85
revenue from film exports, 22
satellite, 52, 53
television program exports, 40, 84–85
Free flow doctrine, 62–63, 64
Free trade, 130, 156
French language market, 86, 87, 112

Gandhi, 21
General Agreement on Trade and Tariffs
   (GATT), 2, 10, 129–134, 136, 140–141,
   154–155, 156, 161
General System of Preferences (GSP), 158
Geneva Phonogram Convention (1972),
   10, 145–146
German language market, 86
GNP, 86–87
Goods versus services trade-offs, 157–158
Government monopsony, 111, 162
Government controls, 9, 10–11, 89–97,
   121–122
Government role in television
   programming trade flows, 49–52, 67
Greece, 105–106, 110, 113
Grenada, 104
GSP Removal Act, 19, 166 n.9
Guatemala, 110
Guinea, 110

Haiti, 18, 104
HBO, 104
Hegemony paradigm, 62–63, 64–65
Hillman, Ayre, L., 118
Hindi/Urdu, 86
Home video markets, 26
Hong Kong, 7, 17, 18, 41, 85

Import restrictions, 106–107, 113, 155
Income, per capita, 4, 85, 87
India: motion picture industry, 7, 18, 84
   trade barriers, 102, 106, 108, 109, 110,
   111, 115 n.11
Indonesia, 105, 106, 108, 113
Intellectual property protection, 99–105,
   122–124, 153, 154–155, 156, 163–164
   Berne and UCC agreements, 142–143
International Frequency Registration
   Board (IFRB), 50

International Telecommunications
   Satellite Organization (INTELSAT), 52
International Telecommunications
   Union (ITU), 50–52
International Television Almanac (1985),
   23
International Trade Commission (ITC),
   132
Invisible operations, 134
Iraq, 65, 111, 112
Ireland, 87, 103
Italy, 52
   attendance figures, 18
   motion picture industry, 17, 84, 137
   private, commercial television
      broadcast systems, 50, 79, 88, 91, 95
   production budgets, 87, 88
   revenue figures for film exports, 22
   trade barriers, 102, 105, 106, 108, 109

Jamaica, 104
Jamaica Broadcasting Company, 104
Japan, 45, 49, 64, 65, 85, 87, 102, 109
   GNP, 86, 87
   private, commercial television broadcast
      systems, 50, 95
   revenues from U.S. films, 19–20
   television programming exports, 40, 85

Kennedy Round, 119
Kenya, 110, 111
Krugman, Paul, 81 n.11
Kuwait, 115 n.6

Language handicap, 75–76
Latin America: film imports, 17, 40, 41,
   46
   private, commercial television
      broadcast systems, 49–50, 95, 96
   television programming exports, 46
   television imports from U.S., 40, 41,
      44–45, 96–97
Leotard, François, 127 n.9
Les Comperes, 23
License fees on TV sets and VCRs
   (France), 109
Linguistic markets, 9, 66, 68, 83–98
   language handicap, 75–76
Loans, grants, and prizes, 109

Local work requirements, 108, 121
Los Santos Inocentes, 20–21
Luxembourg, 50, 91

Mandarin language, 97 n.3
Market access, 154–155, 158–161
Market size; and film quality, 75
  and production budgets, 68–70
Markets, foreign, 26–33
  with different languages, 74–77
  with noncommercial buyers, 77–79
Marvel, Howard, P., 119
*Mass Communications and American
  Empire* (Schiller), 62–63
Mexico, 17, 45
  audiences for U.S. television programs,
    96
  commercial television broadcast
    systems, 95–96
  television programming exports, 41,
    46, 96
  trade barriers, 103, 105, 108, 109, 111
Middle East, 18, 40, 52
Morocco, 110, 111
Most favored nation (MFN) principle,
  129–130, 133–134, 141, 156–157
Motion Picture Association of America
  (MPAA), 1
Motion Picture Export Association of
  America (MPEAA), 45, 122–123
  and trade barriers, 99–110
  passim, 115 n.6
Motion picture industry, 7–8, 13–36
  attendance and revenue figures, 18–22
  exceptions in GATT and OECD,
    136–137
  major exporters of films, 84–85
  number of films produced and traded,
    14–18
  subsidies, 109
  trade restrictions, 105–106, 106–107,
    111
Motion pictures, televised, 46
Murdoch, Rupert, 54
Musicals and variety programs, televised,
  46

*National Treatment for Foreign Control
  Enterprises*, 135

National treatment provision, 130–131,
  135, 136, 137, 142–143, 158–161
Nationalism and culture, 118, 136,
  163–164
NBC, 46
Netherlands, 18, 52, 54, 104, 109, 110
Nevis, 104
New Zealand, 87, 108
News programs, televised, 46
Nicaragua, 110
Nigeria, 110, 112
Nondiscrimination principle, 129–130,
  132–133, 136
Nonresident block account, 110
Nontariff barriers (NTBs), 1, 9, 10,
  117–127
Nordenstreng, Kaarle, 40
NORDSAT, 52
North American Regional Conference on
  DBS Allotments (1983), 50
Northern Africa, 18, 52
Norway, 52, 109, 110

OECD, 10, 134–135, 136–137, 155, 161
Olympic Games, 37

Pakistan, 105, 108, 111
Parallel imports, 113, 160
Pay per transaction, 166 n.12
Pay television, 26
Peltzman, Sam, 118
Philippines, 4, 105, 108, 110, 164–165 n.1
Political economy theories of NTBs, 10,
  117–127
Population size, 4, 86
Portugal, 94, 108, 109, 110, 112
Portuguese Film Institute, 112
Portuguese language market, 46
Post-importation charges, 133
Print production restrictions, 121
Print theft, 102
Private goods, 3
Producers, domestic, 118, 122, 125,
  162–163
Production budgets, 63–64, 68
  and linguistic markets, 87–89
  and market size, 68–70
  and trade barriers, 124–125
  in U.S., 63–64, 87

Production subsidies, 109
Profit maximization, 69, 121
Protectionism, 118, 119, 126, 130, 138, 143, 161–162, 164
Public good components, 2–7, 13, 38, 66, 77
Public presentation, unauthorized, 102
Puerto Rico, 46

Quantitative restrictions, 105–106, 113, 120
Quebec, 112

Radio Audizone Italiana (RAI), 139
Ray, Edward J., 119
Receive-only (RO) stations, 104
Regional television trading areas, 41
Regulation model, 118–119
Revenue figures
imported films, 19–22
public/private television broadcast stations, 91–95
Right of establishment, 158–161
Rogers, E.M., 96
Runaway production, 64
Russian language, 97 n.3

Sacchi, Giuseppe, 139
Sacchi case, 139
St. Kitts, 104
St. Lucia, 104
St. Martin, 104
Satellite associations, regional, 52
Satellite distribution, 7, 52–53
Satellite "footprints," 54
Satellite orbital slot allotment, 50–52
Satellite signals, theft of, 104, 126
Brussels Satellite Convention, 146–147
Satellite-to-home services, 53
Saudi Arabia, 112, 115 n.6, 165 n.6
Scandinavia, 52
Schement, Jorge, 65, 67–68, 79 n.1
Schiller, Herbert, 62
Screen quotas, 105–106
Sequencing of releases, 121, 123, 159–160
Service contracts, 133
Services trade, 2, 131. See also Trade agreements
Signal overspill, 38–39, 54

Singapore, 108
SKY Channel, 54
SMATV, 59 n.22
Sound-recording piracy, 145–146
South Africa, 40, 102, 103, 109
South Korea, 65, 105, 106, 109, 112, 113
Southeast Asia, 18, 41
Soviet Union, 111
GNP, 97 n.3
motion picture industry, 7, 17, 18, 85
television experts, 41
Spain: film revenues, 20–21
televised program exports, 46
trade barriers, 102, 105, 106, 108–109
Spanish International Network (SIN), 41, 46, 65
Spanish-language market, 46, 86, 87
in U.S., 41, 67
Sports programs, televised, 46
Sri Lanka, 105, 106, 110, 111
Stalson, Helena, 165 n.4, 165–166 n.8
Standards code, 133
State enterprises, 132–133
Stigler, George, J., 118
Structural requirements, 4, 67
Subscription television (STV), 59 n.22
Subsidies, 109, 113, 118, 164
Sweden, 52, 109
Switzerland, 54, 106, 109, 137
Syria, 106–107, 111

Taiwan. See China, Republic of
Tanzania, 110
Target audience, 67
Taxes, local/state, 109
Telenovelas, 46
Televisa, 11, 46
Television audiences for imported programs, 41–45
Television broadcast signals, theft of, 104–105, 146–147
Television broadcast systems: budgets, 91
national, 49–50, 111
private, commercial, 49–50, 91–96
public, nonprofit, 49, 50, 77–79, 90–91
state-owned, 49, 65, 90–91
Television broadcasting, transborder, 38–39, 54, 137

Television programming trade,
international, 8, 37–59, 137
   cable television, 53–55
   local programming content
      requirements, 112
   major suppliers, 85
   program flows, 37–45
   quantitative restrictions, 106
   role of governments, 49–52
   satellite distribution, 52–53
   types of programs traded, 46
Television set license fees (France), 109
Television Without Frontiers, 137
Thailand, 108, 111
Third World, 16, 49, 62–63, 64, 65, 114
   and copyright law, 143–144
   satellite orbital slot allotments, 50–52
Tokyo Round (1979), 133–134, 154, 156
Trade agreements, 10, 129–151
   Berne and UCC agreements on
      intellectual property, 142–144
   bilateral and multilateral trade
      agreements, 129, 131, 141–142
   copyright agreements, 144–145,
      145–147
   EEC, 137–141, 144–145
   film industry exceptions in GATT and
      OECD, 136–137
   GATT, 129–134
   OECD codes, 134–135
Trade and Tariff Act (1984), 99, 129
Trade barriers, 9, 10, 89, 99–116
   active/passive, 153–156. *See also*
      Nontariff barriers (NTBs)
Trade dispute settlement procedures,
   131–132, 161
Trade reform, 163–164
Transborder television broadcasting,
   38–39, 54, 137
Transparency principle, 132, 135, 161
Treaty of Rome, 138–139, 144, 150 n.54
Trinidad, 104, 110
Turkey, 110
Turner, Ted, 46
Twentieth Century Fox, 20

UHF converters, 67
UNESCO, 63, 142
   survey data, 14, 40–41, 78, 169

Uniform Copyright Convention, 10
United Kingdom, 40, 52, 87
   attendance figures, 18
   motion picture industry, 85, 137
   private, commercial broadcast systems,
      50, 91, 95
   trade barriers, 102, 103, 105, 106, 109
United Nations, 62, 63, 142. *See also*
   International Telecommunications
   Union; (ITU); UNESCO; World
   Intellectual Property Organization
   (WIPO)
United States: admission prices, 4
   attendance and revenue figures for
      visual exports, 18–22
   and Berne/UCC agreements, 142, 154
   and Brussels Satellite Convention, 147
   cable television, 41, 95
   commercial television, 91–95
   distribution companies, restrictions on,
      112
   dollar, 30
   domestic revenue figures, 95
   economic analysis of video trade,
      62–66
   foreign film market, 8, 22–26, 27–30,
      98
   home video market, 26
   independent filmmakers, 32–33, 36
      n.12
   Latin America, diminishing audiences
      for U.S. television programs in, 96
   motion picture industry, 1, 7–8, 13–35
      passim, 36 n.10
   population size/GNP, 87
   private, commercial television
      broadcast systems, 50
   production budgets, 63–64, 87
   public/private television budgets/
      revenues, 91
   relationship between film and
      television production, 89–90
   Spanish-language television in, 41
   television industry, 8, 40–41, 46
   and UNESCO, 63
U.S. Chamber of Commerce (Taipei), 107
U.S.-Israeli multi-sector agreement, 149
   n.42, 165 n.5
U.S. National Study, 132, 135, 141

U.S. Trade Representative (USTR), 99, 107, 109, 160. *See also U.S. National Study*, 132, 135, 141
Universal Copyright Convention (UCC), 142–144

Variety, 4
Varis, Tapio, 40–41
Venezuela, 56, 110, 120
Video piracy, 122–124, 162
  and Brussels Satellite Convention, 146
  costs to industry, 1, 102, 122
  and EEC, 113
  and GATT, 154
  market shares achieved by, 103
  and MFN principle, 157
  and NTBs, 125–126
  and OECD, 155
  in Saudi Arabia, 115 n.6, 165 n.6
  in Taiwan, 107
  technology of, 7, 31
Videocassette recorders (VCRs), 26
  license fees, 109
Videocassettes, 26
  revenues, 26
  tax on blank cassettes, 109
  unauthorized, imports of, 103–104

Virgin Gorda, 104

Warner, 20
West Germany, 18, 65, 85, 102, 106
  DBS satellite, 53
  television programming exports, 40, 85
Western Europe, 41, 64, 65, 102
  attendance figures, 18
  cable television, 53–54, 95
  cable television news program imports, 46
  ESA satellite, 52
  film rental terms, 110
  motion picture industry, 18, 24–25
  public, nonprofit television systems, 49, 79, 91
  subsidies, 112
  television program imports from U.S., 40, 46, 96–97
  television revenue/budgets (public/commercial), 91, 95
  video piracy, 112–113
World Administrative Radio Conference (WARC) (1979), 50–52
World Intellectual Property Organization (WIPO), 142
WTBS, 104

ABOUT THE AUTHORS

Steven S. Wildman is a senior economist with the consulting firm of Economists Incorporated. Dr. Wildman provides consulting advice on a variety of policy topics, including antitrust, regulation, competition, and trade in media and telecommunications industries. He was previously an assistant professor in the Department of Economics at UCLA and a consultant to the Rand Corporation. He held a National Science Foundation Fellowship from 1974 to 1977. Dr. Wildman has published a number of articles and papers on competition in the broadcasting industries and other communications-related issues. He holds a B.A. from Wabash College and a Ph.D. in economics from Stanford University.

Stephen E. Siwek is a senior consultant with Economists Incorporated, Washington, D.C. He specializes in financial and economic analysis, with particular emphasis on communications industries. He has appeared as an expert witness before U.S. federal and state regulatory agencies on more than thirty occasions. He has acted as a consultant to numerous telecommunications and media corporations in connection with regulatory, antitrust, and general business matters and has also provided advice and analysis to various importer associations appearing before the U.S. International Trade Commission. Prior to joining Economists Incorporated, he held the position of senior consultant with Snavely, King and Associates Inc., a Washington, D.C.-based economic consulting firm.

Mr. Siwek holds a B.A. degree in economics from Boston College and an M.B.A. degree in finance and marketing from the George Washington University.